PAY LESS
KEEP WARM

OPTIMA

PAY LESS
KEEP WARM

Hundreds of Ways to
Save on Fuel Bills

BARTY PHILLIPS

ILLUSTRATED BY ROS ASQUITH

An OPTIMA book

First published in 1987 by
Macdonald Optima, a division of
Macdonald & Co. (Publishers) Ltd

A BPCC PLC company

British Library Cataloguing in Publication Data

Phillips, Barty
    Pay less keep warm.
    1. Dwellings——Insulation——Amateurs'
    manuals
    I. Title
    693.8'32   TH1715

    ISBN 0-356-12889-X

Macdonald & Co. (Publishers) Ltd
3rd Floor
Greater London House
Hampstead Road
London NW1 7QX

Printed and bound in Great Britain by
The Guernsey Press Co. Ltd., Guernsey, Channel Islands.

My grateful thanks to John Phillips who did much of the research for this book. And thanks too to NATTA for helping with information and slides, to Jervis Read for giving me the idea in the first place, to my sister Rosamund for helping me pin the carpet felt to my roof all those years ago which prevented the tank from freezing up yet again and to Phil Glynn for insulating my loft so that even the bathroom feels warm now.

CONTENTS

CONTENTS

INTRODUCTION

There has been a lot of talk about insulation and energy saving in the last few years and there are plenty of books to tell you how to insulate your loft efficiently and how to find somebody to fill your cavity wall with urea formaldehyde foam. Other books tell you about alternative forms of heating and the state of research into them. There are also excellent leaflets produced by local communities and organisations advising those in need of their statutory rights and how to claim for benefits and allowances.

The trouble is, it is hard to find all this information in the same place. It is equally hard to get a complete picture of the reasons why we must try so hard to save energy. This book aims to provide a general view of what we can expect of our fuels in the future, how we can preserve them so as to give ourselves time to provide alternatives, and most important of all, how to keep warm and cosy at home whilst saving money on fuel bills.

This is not a technical book, nor is it a DIY book. It points the way to doing a great deal yourself to making your home more comfortable, your fuel bills cheaper and prolonging the life of our precious fossil fuels.

1.
WHY BOTHER TO SAVE ENERGY?

Ten years ago the government organised its first campaign to get people to save fuel: the 'Save It' campaign. In 1986 it launched the 'Monergy' campaign with the same intention but a little more bite, putting the emphasis on insulation so that less heat could escape and therefore less would have to be generated (and paid for) to keep people warm and snug in their homes.

But why should we bother to save energy? What can individuals do that could possibly make any difference? In fact we can do a great deal and what we do makes a great difference not just to ourselves, but to the next generation coming up. Think of them too.

First of all, the world is running out of fossil fuels. Oil and gas have been estimated to last for only another 20 years or so. Coal may give us another 150 years but we have not yet found a really safe or efficient alternative. So it is very much in our interests to use as little fuel as we possibly can while still keeping warm and comfortable.

Secondly, saving energy will save you money. Did you know that we in Britain use a greater proportion of our total fuel consumption for domestic heating than any other country in Europe? And our homes are still colder than the Europeans'. Because our homes are so poorly insulated, most of the heat we pay for goes straight out again to pointlessly heat the outside air. In fact, in most British homes three quarters of our heating disappears in this way. For every £100 you spend on your heating bills, £75 is completely wasted and you are only benefitting from £25's worth of heat. We are literally throwing money away.

There are 18 million homes in England and Wales alone, and of those only a very few conform to the minimum standards laid down by the 1965 building regulations (which instruct that a laughably inadequate 2.5 cm (1 in) of insulating material should be used in the roof space of a home). Even fewer conform to the 1975 regulations which raised that minimum to 5 cm (2 in). It's not as though Britain were a warm country either. In Scandinavia, where they acknowledge their cold winters, they think it worthwhile to put in 10-15 cm (4-6 in) thick insulation as a rule and in Sweden often as much as 25 cm (10 in). Scandinavian heating costs are minimal and yet their comfort is well known.

Although it will never be possible to eliminate all loss of heat, we can reduce wastage considerably by insulating with thermal materials in our homes. Even if we adopt only the cheap and easy measures, we can still reduce the heating costs of our homes by half. In most family homes this means a saving of around £100 or more a year, which would cover the cost of most basic insulation in three or four years. Some techniques, however, begin to pay for themselves immediately.

Thirdly, an efficiently insulated home will not have to be decorated so often. When condensation forms indoors, particularly on old surfaces, it causes the deterioration of any paint or paper on them. Insulation and ventilation can cut condensation a good deal. If you have just decorated your home, by insulating it you postpone the need to redecorate as the paint and wallpaper last longer. Dirt tends to cling to cool surfaces so you find that an insulated house stays cleaner longer than an uninsulated one. Condensation can also rot window frames and damage the fabric of the building, so preventing it actually protects your home.

Fourthly, because less fuel is used in insulated homes, less pollution of the environment occurs through the burning of gas, oil, coal and other fuels so fewer toxic fumes escape into the air. Pollution of the environment, not just from chemical emissions of factory chimneys and the emptying of toxic waste into rivers but also from the burning of refuse in municipal dumps which can be highly poisonous, has become increasingly worrying. The less we contribute to that, the better.

Fifthly, by saving energy we can save lives. Both young children and the elderly are susceptible to the cold. Many old people are more frightened of running up huge fuel bills that they will not be able to pay than they are of the cold itself. There are many very simple ways in which relatives and friends can help old people to keep warm and use less fuel.

Lastly, an insulated home is warmer, more comfortable and healthier than an uninsulated one. Most bodies maintain a temperature of 37°C (98.4°F) but people can feel perfectly comfortable in considerably lower air temperatures, providing the surrounding structures are well insulated and reflect back the radiant heat given out by bodies and radiant heaters in the room. If you have comprehensive insulation at home, you will find that by heating just the living room, you can move freely about the house without suffering the sudden chill which hits you if you walk into an uninsulated room.

For instance, the bedroom will stay warm without the need to have an expensive electric fire on just before bedtime. When you get up in the morning, your insulated home acts like a giant storage heater, keeping in the heat and taking the edge off the chilly mornings. The cosiness is enhanced by the fact that a thermally insulated home is also, to a certain extent, an acoustically insulated home. While shutting out the cold and keeping in the warm, you also shut out many of the noises from outside, making your house like a cocoon and covering it in what is effectively a warm duvet.

This works on the same principle as the traditional 'hay box' method of cooking in which a well insulated pan continues to cook porridge or stew all night even when taken off the heat. You will see, if you try, that insulation can be nothing short of miraculous. The hay box method was used by people in the days when cooking stoves would die out during the night. The pan was heated initially and then placed in a 'nest' of hay where it continued cooking for hours. Soldiers used this method during the war and a friend of my mother's used to cook her lunch every day in a chest of old fabrics. I have tried it with a sag bag chair and it worked perfectly.

INSULATION PAYS

You can keep as warm — or warmer — by generating a little heat and keeping it in as you can by generating a lot of heat and letting most of it escape. If we all insulated our homes, hundreds of millions of pounds could be saved.

Obviously the most effective thing you can do is to insulate the whole house — like putting a tea cosy on a teapot or the double skin round a vacuum flask. Any gaps will allow heat to escape and ruin the effect. Some methods are much cheaper and easier to do than others and if you begin with those you will have made a good start. The very great difference to your comfort and your bank balance may encourage you to carry on with the more expensive procedures. The secret is to go about things in the right order.

You should deal with insulation the very moment you move into a new home, or decide to do any conversion or decorating work on your present one. If you are about to install a new central heating system it is absolutely essential to insulate first, because then you will need a smaller boiler which uses less fuel. Too large a system not only wastes money and fuel, but is also uncomfortably hot. Remember that three quarters of the energy you are paying for is doing absolutely nothing at all.

Some methods of insulation are more cost effective than others and there is definitely a sensible order to go about things. Indeed, be warned. Any old insulation is not necessarily better than none at all and some forms of insulating, such as double glazing throughout the house, will probably never pay for themselves in your lifetime. Cavity wall insulation, for example, is an extremely effective but costly heat barrier and can take a good few years before it begins to pay for itself. If it is badly installed, it can cause more trouble than savings and you may have to pay for a damp proofing specialist to correct the damage.

Draughtproofing

The very cheapest and quickest procedure, and therefore the most immediately rewarding, is draughtproofing. In the days before I knew anything about insulating or worried about the state of the paintwork, I went right round my home and taped up every window and door with a roll of sticky tape until I could feel no more draughts coming through. This made such a difference to our comfort that I have kept it up ever since, learning to buy foam strip so that the paint would not peel off with the sticky tape come the spring. My house is old and very draughty and this simple two-hour operation has saved me countless pounds and many draughty evenings, for practically no financial outlay at all. It is estimated that only ten per cent of your heating escapes through small gaps in window and door frames etc, but this is ten per cent which you can save immediately on the very next bill if you stop them up. You will be astonished to discover how much cosier your home will be when you have done it.

Roof

The obvious next step, and a very straightforward one, is to insulate the roof space. In most homes, losses through the roof account for 15-30 per cent of all the heat that escapes. In a bungalow, which has a comparatively large roof space, the loss is even greater — less, of course, if you live in one of the middle storeys of a block of flats.

In most homes the roof is used only as storage space and insulation is laid on top of or between the floor joists in the loft. This is an easy procedure, though it can be an uncomfortable task, and it is not worth paying for a professional to do something that is so easy to do yourself.

If the space is tall enough to be used as a room, you will have to put the insulation on the inside of the roof itself. This is a bit more expensive and slightly more difficult to fix but just as worthwhile, even if you pay someone to do it for you. Loft insulation should pay for itself in about three years. You can get a grant for insulating your roof and for buying a jacket for the hot water cylinder (see page 85). When I had my loft insulated, I could not at first understand why the bathroom was so warm. I thought someone had been having a bath. But no, it was the rock wool above keeping the warmth from the hot water cylinder in.

With these two simple and cheap procedures, instant draughtproofing and loft insulation, you will already have saved about half the warmth which has been escaping from your home. From now on, any more insulation becomes an expensive item and takes longer to pay for itself, though most of it is probably worth doing in the long run.

Walls

A lot of a home's heat is lost through the walls, about 20-35 per cent of the total loss. Of course, if you live in a terraced house you are already insulated on either side by the houses next door, and if you live in the middle storeys of a tall building, you will be insulated above and below by your neighbours. Nevertheless, plenty of heat still escapes through the outside walls — especially if you live in a detached house.

Most post-war houses have cavity walls, consisting of two 11.5 cm (4½in) walls with a 5 cm (2in) gap between them. These lose less heat than older ones which usually have solid 23 cm (9in) brick walls. Modern cavity walls have a slab of insulating material built into them. You cannot put that in after the house has been built so if you have unfilled cavity walls, it is best to insulate by having thermal material injected into the gap. Holes are drilled into the outer skin of the brick wall and then the insulation is injected under pressure.

This is definitely not a DIY job and the British Standards Institution has set standards for both the materials and the installation of most types of cavity wall insulation. Choose a firm which has registered under this scheme and check that materials and techniques used have been approved by the Agrement Board. Make sure that the contractor has an Agrement Board Certificate, which you should ask to see so that you can be certain of getting a good job done.

Various materials are used for cavity wall fillings. There is urea formaldehyde foam which is a mixture of formaldehyde resin, hardener and water. As this mixture is injected into the wall, the resin foams up inside the cavity and sets hard. The material and the air trapped in it give excellent insulation.

Foam is not always suitable for all types of wall. If any of your walls are made of weatherboard or Dutch tiles, for instance, you may be able to use it, but you will have to get local authority permission first. The contractor should do this for you.

Other types of insulation filler include expanded polystyrene beads and mineral fibre which are blown in under pressure. Do not forget that the cavity may have heavy electric cables running through it, for example, for supplying electricity to the cooker, immersion heater or storage heaters. Warn the contractor about these, because it is best not to insulate them too much in case they overheat.

Most homes built before 1940 have solid walls. You can still insulate such walls by fitting insulating materials to the outside of the house or the inside. Professionally done, this costs more than cavity wall insulation and, since any outside treatment is going to affect the look of the house, you must get permission from the local council before going ahead. Exterior changes may not comply with local bye-laws and if your home is listed as being of particular historic interest, you almost certainly will not get permission.

Insulating inside the house is usually more effective than outside anyway. The insulation material forms a barrier which reduces the amount of heat absorbed by the walls, so the room heats up quite quickly — it also cools down slowly. Thermal insulation fixed to the inside walls is cheaper to install than on outside walls and you can spread the cost by doing one room at a time. But you will, of course, make the room smaller and have to alter the position of window sills, door frames, electric points, switches and so on. You also have to redecorate when you've finished. Unless you are an extremely keen DIYer or builder, or have plenty of time on your hands, get a professional in to do the work.

There are two basic methods. You can either make a timber framework, fit plasterboard sheets to that and fill the cavity with insulating material such as glass fibre or rock wool or expanded polystyrene sheets — or you can stick thermal board onto the existing wall. The walls must be sound and free from damp before you start the work.

There are plenty of other, less efficient but equally worthwhile ways of insulating inside which are a great deal easier and cheaper to apply (see page 53).

Floors
You lose 10-20 per cent of heat from floors and most of that is through the ground floor. Insulating the floor can be a perfectly possible DIY job, though if you want to get right under the floor and insulate beneath the floorboards, it could be a job for a builder. Various cheap and quick suggestions are to be found in chapter 4.

By insulating the ceiling you make the room smaller and therefore it costs less to heat. You may also, specially in older houses, be able to lower a high and uneven ceiling, conceal pipes and so on. But building regulations state that there should never be less than 2.3 m (7 ft 6 in) between floor and ceiling. You can either make a timber frame and fit sheets of plasterboard or thermal board to this, or fix a lightweight aluminium framework suspended from the ceiling and insert insulation tiles into it. Kits are available for this but it is a job only for people with a practical streak and time on their hands.

USE FUELS WISELY

Besides insulation, one of the easiest ways to save on heating bills without decreasing your home comfort is to use fuels wisely. There are many things you can do, such as initiating basic energy saving habits at home by switching off unwanted lights and closing doors. Various devices can also be bought to control and maximise the use of your central heating system.

Firstly, make sure you have an efficient heating system and one that is right for your particular home and way of life. Choose the system after you have insulated because you will need a substantially smaller boiler, and perhaps radiators, than you did before. Even if you do not want to change all the radiators, if your boiler is more than five years old, it is almost certainly worth buying a neater and more efficient one.

If you are getting a new heating system installed, check that you have the most efficient controls for it. A central thermostat should be placed so that it reflects heat where you most need it — not out in the hall. A programmer can be very helpful if you are out all day. It turns the heating on before you get up, off again when you have gone to work, on again in the evening just before you get home and off again after you have gone to bed. However, if your home suffers from condensation, you might prefer to have a day/night thermostat which turns the heating down when you do not need it on full and keeps the chill off all the time.

Dimmer switches on lights save quite a lot of electricity and do not wear out the bulb any quicker than normal use. There are many other gadgets which help to reduce fuel consumption. Most modern designs of electrical equipment take into account the saving of energy but just as important is the state of mind that remembers to use them.

As a mother instinctively learns to turn saucepan handles inwards when she has young children, you can learn to instinctively turn off lights which are not being used, or to close doors firmly when leaving or coming into a room. 'Were you born in a barn?' was the constant cry of adults when I was a young girl in Scotland, because every time you opened the door a fierce gale swept in. Now I instinctively close doors wherever I go.

2.
UNDERSTANDING HEAT

An understanding of where heat comes from, where it goes and how it moves in your home helps you to decide where and what sort of heating and insulation you need. There is no doubt that you feel warmer in a coolish room which is well insulated than huddling in front of an electric bar fire in a freezing room, where you are not keeping warm efficiently.

HEAT LOSS

Heat transfer always occurs from the warmer thing to the cooler one until their temperatures are equal. The greater the temperature difference, the faster the heat is transferred. Human comfort is affected by the way heat is transferred and not simply by the actual temperature in a room. This means that you feel colder when standing next to a large window than in another part of the room at the same temperature because the heat from your body is being 'sucked' out by the cold of the glass.

Heat moves in three specific ways round the house, by conduction, convection and radiation.

Conduction
Heat is conducted either along or through a material or from one material to another. Some materials conduct heat better than others. For instance heat moves quickly from the inside of an uninsulated wall to the cold outside. Insulation materials should therefore be made so as to decrease the rate of conduction. As air is a poor conductor

of heat, insulation materials often have air pockets within their structure. Water, on the other hand, conducts heat extremely well and damp considerably lessens the efficiency of an insulating material. So one of the important aspects of insulation is damp proofing.

Convection

Air which is heated becomes lighter and tends to rise. If a house is draughty, cold air from the draughts moves in to take the place of the warm air. Meanwhile, the warm air rises up through the ceiling to disappear through the roof. In winter a well insulated house keeps a little hat of snow whereas badly insulated ones have snow-free roofs, and all the heat you have paid for goes to melt the snow unnecessarily. A combination of loft insulation and draughtproofing makes an enormous difference to how much heat you lose through convection.

Radiation

Surfaces of warm objects send rays of heat energy in all directions, so that the hotter objects give their heat to the cooler ones facing them. This is radiation. Warmth from radiators or heaters will literally 'radiate' out through the fabric of a house. You can feel the effect of a large, cold surface such as a pane of glass because your body radiates its heat in that direction. As heat reflects from bright surfaces, the thing to do is send it right back inside by using a sheet of aluminium foil or other reflective material on the wall, specially behind radiators. This keeps the warmth in. Bright, light paints and wallpapers (brilliant white is ideal) will also lessen the amount of heat lost in this way.

CONDENSATION

Because of the humidity of our climate, condensation can be a problem. Condensation is caused by warm air meeting a cold surface — the moisture in the air cools rapidly and condenses on the surface in tiny water droplets. It is usually found on the insides of windows and walls or ceilings with cold inside surfaces, particularly those in bathrooms and kitchens where there is more moisture. The condition is always worse in insufficiently heated and badly ventilated homes. In time it causes damage to the paintwork, woodwork and plaster.

There are three things needed to cure condensation: good insulation of structural surfaces, efficient background heating to prevent those surfaces from getting cold and to allow them to absorb back some of the moisture and good ventilation. It is no good providing one or two of these, you need all three. Insulation of various parts of the house is described in the following chapters and some guidelines on heating systems can be found in chapter 6.

The best way to prevent permanent condensation is not to allow the room ever to get absolutely cold. If you have central heating use a day/night thermostat to turn the heating down, but not off, rather than a programmer which turns the heating off completely for certain periods.

If you do not have central heating, you can fit a small, low level storage heater or 300 or 400 watt electric skirting heater and leave it on continuously. This should not be expensive to run but will contribute enormously to your comfort. Top up with a fan or radiant heater when you are in the room.

Moisture prevention

You can try to prevent too much moisture from coming into the house in the first place. Condensation is often caused by moisture from washing or cooking where a room is badly ventilated. In the kitchen, an extractor fan solves the problem and is cheaply and easily installed.

These are some general things you can do to reduce the amount of moisture created in your home:

1. Set the thermostat on the hot water cylinder to 60°C (140°F) which will not scald the user and reduces the amount of steam.
2. Use a pressure cooker.
3. Do not let the kettle boil longer than necessary.
4. In the bathroom, turn on the cold water tap to the bath before turning on the hot tap.
5. Install an extractor fan. The size you need depends on the volume of the room. Set it in the wall rather than a window if you can. It is quieter that way because the wall absorbs the vibration. It should also, preferably, be positioned just above the source of the steam, for example, near the cooker or bath.
6. Avoid paints, papers and tiles with glossy surfaces. Use matt, semi-matt or textured surfaces which temporarily mop up condensing moisture until it is absorbed back into the room.
7. Open windows for a short time before you start cooking. Keep draughtproofed doors closed to prevent cold air moving through the house.

N.B. Paraffin heaters and gas heaters make condensation worse. They produce a gallon of water vapour for every gallon of fuel used.

Damp proofing

Obviously the damper your house is, the more you will suffer from condensation. The more you suffer from condensation the less efficient your insulation is going to be. If the problem is really bad there are a number of damp proofing techniques available to you.

A damp proofing material can be 'infused' into a solid wall through small holes distributed throughout the structure. You can get the wall damp proofed by 'electro-osmosis' which works like a lightning conductor and draws water via copper strips down into the ground. This is suitable for a basement with earth underneath it. Alternatively use 'impervious rendering' in which a chemical is mixed with plaster to form a waterproof coat for walls and ceilings or bituminous lath (wooden planks with tarred coating), which can be fixed to the walls with rust proof nails to form a cavity, isolating the damp and forming a key for plaster. All these techniques must be professionally applied.

VENTILATION THROUGH THE HOUSE

It is the pressure around a house caused by wind and turbulence, coupled with the position of the gaps in the house's structure, which dictate the patterns of ventilation or draught through your home.

In a constantly warm house, little ventilation is needed. An open window, for instance, in a cold season brings in far too much air. One answer is to leave a window open while everyone is out, but you do not want to encourage burglars, and some home insurance policies demand closed windows in empty houses. You can, of course, fix extractor fans in the windows or doors, but they are often unsightly.

A better solution is something called 'trickle ventilation' which works on the principle that a very small amount of air is allowed into the house at a constant rate. The air flow is controlled so that when a gale blows up outside the ventilation device can be shut off, or when a room becomes stuffy or full of cigarette smoke it can be opened up to disperse the moisture and smell at a steady rate.

These ventilators hardly affect heat loss and are designed to be fitted into the opening sashes of good timber windows. A line of holes is bored through the timber and a narrow sliding aluminium strip with corresponding holes is fitted over that. (You can buy these from DIY shops.) The holes can then be exposed, partially covered or closed in the same way as the lid of a talcum powder cannister.

You should allow about 15 sq cm (2½ sq in) of ventilator area to every 3 sq m (100 sq ft) of room area, though large rooms with two or more outside walls need less and enclosed or small stuffy rooms more. There is no harm in opening windows from time to time if you like, but you should not have to open them from the ventilation point of view.

If there is unnecessary ventilation in your home, for instance in an uninsulated loft space, suction currents are most likely to occur at the roof, pulling warm air out of the house. Cold draughts coming in from under the doors and floorboards will also have a similar effect. You can drastically reduce such wasteful and constant heat loss with thorough draughtproofing and insulating all round the house.

3.
QUICK AND BASIC DRAUGHTPROOFING

The first and most important step to take in reducing your heating bills is to insulate your house against heat loss. After insulation, a house loses only 43 per cent of the heat it would have lost before. The most essential insulation can be done quickly, easily and, above all, cheaply so you can reduce your heating bills on a very small initial outlay. Immediate savings will show on your next fuel bill, and at the same time your home comfort is noticeably increased.

It is reckoned that something between 10 and 20 per cent of heat loss of a whole house can be accounted for by draughts, but this varies depending on the age and condition of your home. In an old house, where the woodwork has warped, cracks have appeared and general wear and tear has produced gaps and holes which are not highly visible, draughts will be a major problem.

The normal clearance between doors and windows and their frames is about 2.5 mm (⅛in). Taken all together, this could amount to a 1.2 sq m (4 sq ft) hole in your house, enough to make you very cold indeed on a bitter windy day. However, in most old houses the situation is worse still. Door and window frames will almost certainly have warped and/or shrunk so that the gaps are much larger. In fact, homes do not have to be so very old before this happens. So you can see why draughts are things to be taken seriously.

Draughtproofing is by far the cheapest form of insulation, giving the quickest return in energy conservation and, therefore, savings on fuel bills. You can probably go round and seal the whole house in one day or perhaps an evening, and the materials are cheap and readily available.

Go round your home with a lighted candle and you will be surprised at the amount of draught blowing the flame in all directions. Just holding the back of your hand up to doors or windows you will be startled at the strength of the cold and how the wind plays onto your fingers. Both these exercises are useful ways of locating draughts.

The worst problems are usually round doors and windows which no longer fit properly, through unused open fireplaces, joins between skirting boards and floors and pipe openings in walls and ceilings. Check the bath waste outlets. Quite a chilly breeze can blow through there when the wind is in the right direction. Do not forget the ceiling hatch into the loft and the letter box, also key holes and door latches.

Once you have isolated the draughty spots, there are various products you can use to stop them up. Most of them you can fix yourself, very cheaply.

DOOR AND WINDOW FRAMES

There are various ways of taping and sealing windows and doors. You will find that many windows can remain closed throughout the winter, which makes taping them up much easier, of course.

As a temporary measure, masking tape across the gaps round window frames, unused doors and the loft hatch will have an immediate effect. Sello or Scotch tape can be used but are not really to be recommended as they tend to take the paint with them when you pull them off. For more permanent draughtproofing and for doors and windows which need to be opened and closed, a variety of products can be bought from your local DIY supplier.

Cheapest and easiest to put on are the rolls of self-adhesive foam strip which you stick around the edges of the frame to fill the gaps. They stick to both metal and wood and are invisible when the doors or windows are closed. However, they are not as durable as other kinds of

strip available. They also tend to get dirty quickly and they will not fill very large gaps. If you do use this kind (and it is certainly the easiest to apply) you will probably have to replace it every couple of years. When fixing anything adhesive, make sure that the paint surface is perfectly clean and dry. If you find a product does not stick very well, you can be pretty sure it is because you have not prepared the surfaces properly.

As an alternative, you can buy plastic strip in the form of a flexible tube. This is fixed to the door frame by a flange (a strip projecting over the face of the door) and when the door closes it squashes the tube, effectively sealing the gap. These are also very cheap but need quite a bit of care when being fixed into place. Read the instructions through before you begin work and then follow them step by step.

There are several types of 'V' shaped strips and strips with sprung hinged flaps, which come either in bronze, copper or plastic. Bronze and copper strips are more durable but most effective on door and window frames which are fairly true, as they do not have enough flexibility to cope with particularly bad irregularities. The V should face outwards on the hinged side of the door and inwards on the other side and the top. Once properly fitted, given the frame is not too distorted, this type of strip will last for years.

Plastic strips are cheaper and more flexible but do not last nearly as long. After about three years you should expect to replace them.

DOORS AND THRESHOLDS

The cheapest and easiest external draught excluder to fix is a plain strip of wood or plastic attached to the door, with an edge of bristles or rubber which brushes against the floor. This type, however, soon wears out due to constant rubbing whenever the door is opened and closed.

Slightly more complex is the hinged type, where the sealing strip swings clear of the floor when the door is opened and locks back into place as the door closes. These tend to last for a couple of years longer than the plain strips and the more sturdy ones are fine for external doors. Like the hinged type, the parallel bar excluders allow the sealing strip to swing clear of the floor when the door is opened. Both of these types require care and time for fixing but last far longer and tend to be more efficient than the plain strip.

Each of these types of strip are fine for internal doors and windows but for external or badly warped doors, you should consider a more durable and effective draught excluder. One type consists of an aluminium strip holding a plastic tube which is fitted to the frame. When the door closes, the tube compresses, forming a tight seal, firm enough to keep out the most insistent draughts. Other types use a flap or bristles instead of the plastic tube and if you are considering the looks of the fixture, you might prefer these as they are less visible. In any case, the extra expense and the care needed in fixing these more durable types will unquestionably pay in the long run and give you effective service over a long period. Do not seal the tops of internal doors. Draughts are not worrying at this height and they bring in some necessary fresh air.

The bottom of the outside front door is quite likely to be the cause of your worst draught problems. There are, again, many ways of dealing with this, ranging from the quick, makeshift solutions where you would use resources close to hand, such as old coats and sticky tape, to the more permanent fixtures which require some careful DIY.

There are a great many ready made draught excluders on the market of varying sizes. Some can be cut to measure. Do not forget to measure the size of your door before you set off to buy one. You should choose one which provides an efficient seal against both the wind and the driven rain and which will last. When you think of the amount of heavy boot and shoe traffic an external door gets, you will see that it needs a more firmly constructed excluder than internal, less heavily used doors which may be fitted with the cheaper draught strips.

An alternative to having the excluder fitted to the door is to have one fixed to the threshold. This is a strip of rubber or foam which is squashed down by the door when it closes. Choose one which you think can stand the punishment from the sort of traffic you normally expect to come through your front door.

Another option is the combination type where one part is attached to the door and the other to the floor. As the door closes, both parts lock into place forming an effective seal. This type is durable and especially effective for keeping out rain, as the part attached to the outside of the door acts as a water bar. A bit more skill is required for fixing this type and, as with the threshold excluder, the bottom of the door may need to be planed down a bit to get the close fitting seal you need, especially for external doors.

THE PORCH

The front and back outside doors of a house, which are at the mercy of wind, rain, fog, smog and dust need the heaviest insulation. An outside porch is a very efficient way to keep draughts out because it provides a large insulating air space and an added barrier. If your house already has a porch, or if you intend to have one built, make sure it is as soundly draughtproofed and waterproofed as the door itself. From the insulation point of view a solid structure with a good roof and door is far and away better than the simple open-framework type. You may, however, need planning permission.

CHEAP AND CHEERFUL

The obvious but effective traditional device of hanging a heavy curtain or blanket across a door or large window can be very helpful.

I'VE A FEELING THEY MEANT THE CURTAIN TO GO INSIDE THE DOOR

One traditional favourite is the 'floor dog'. You can make one of these by stuffing the arm of an old pullover or coat and wedging it between the floor and the door. This will not cost you anything and is an effective immediate measure, but can be inconvenient, especially when stretched out in front of a doorway where people are going in and out all the time. Consider how much of a real hazard such an obstacle may be to very young children and old people who are likely to trip up, either through bad balance or bad eyesight.

Makeshift ideas can, however, be particularly helpful in certain circumstances. Pensioners, for instance, who often sit in front of a single-bar fire in the depths of winter and feel the cold acutely, could benefit tremendously from a little draughtproofing. This is something which could be done for them very easily and cheaply by friends or neighbours, though it might be just more than they could manage on their own.

FIREPLACES

Fireplaces should be blocked off if you do not intend to use them. A considerable amount of heat is lost through thermal currents going up the chimney and cold draughts coming down. A piece of chipboard or plywood cut to the right size can be wedged into place. Even the cardboard from a supermarket box can be used.

If you do not intend to use the fireplace at all, the chimney can be blocked at the top with brick or a piece of slate. A blocked off fire should have an airbrick low down on the outside wall to allow enough ventilation to guard against condensation on the inside wall. Do not block up the flue so permanently that it can never be used again. You, or someone else, may well want to have an open fire. Work done in bricking up the space or fitting an airbrick may irreparably damage the flue so be careful how you go about it.

SKIRTING BOARDS AND FLOORS

A surprising amount of draught can come up through the gaps between floorboards and between the floor and skirting boards in houses which have suspended floors. Carpets alone will not be enough to keep these draughts out. Filling such gaps is likely to be a long and boring job and you may decide it is simply not worth it, particularly if your long-term insulation plan (see chapter 1 page 15) includes laying under-floor insulation anyway. Nevertheless, draughtproofing here will have an immediate effect on your comfort and energy wastage and can be done very cheaply.

You can make your own filler with a mixture of fine sawdust, plaster of Paris and an ounce of decorator's size for each pint. Alternatively, you can make papier mâché from torn newspaper and hot water. When dried, this can be stained to match the shade of the floorboards. Clear up as you go along otherwise you will have to do a lot of planing down afterwards. If the gaps are very wide, over 2.5 mm (1/8 in), you might even glue in slivers of wood which can then be sanded down to the level of the floor.

A neat and effective solution to gaps between skirting and floorboards is to nail strips of quadrant moulding to the base of the skirting once the gaps have been sealed. Again, use papier mâché, home-made or bought mastic to plug the gaps. The moulding can then be painted to match the skirting.

OTHER SOURCES OF DRAUGHT

Test the power points and switches on external walls for draughts with the back of your hand. You may be surprised to find cold air coming in here. If you find it is, switch off the power at the mains before doing anything. Remove the front plate, pull it back from the wall and tape over any gaps you can see. Make sure you do not twist the cable or damage it in the process.

The letter box is often overlooked as a source of draught. But if the flap is at all loose, a considerable wind will blow through. Newspapers or similar sized packages wedged half way in also let in an enormous amount of cold air. You can prevent all that by building a large roomy box and fixing it to the door to collect the letters and to contain the draught.

Cat flaps are very draughty conveniences. Try to find one which closes tightly and stays closed, or provide your cat with a litter tray and persuade it to live indoors during the coldest weather. Tape up the flap in the meantime.

VENTILATION

While carrying out your draughtproofing programme bear in mind that your house does need a certain amount of fresh air. You need ventilation to provide the constant supply of oxygen for people to breathe, to allow combustion heaters to burn their fuel efficiently and supply air flow up the chimney. (This advice does not apply to gas appliances with balanced flues, which draw the air directly from outside.) Oxygen also absorbs the moisture caused by cooking and washing and disperses unpleasant odours like cigarette smoke or burnt toast.

In most homes getting enough fresh air is never going to be a problem. More than enough percolates through the structure of a house in the natural course of events. If you live in a very small area, if the air becomes polluted (with cigarette smoke and so on) or if you have a fuel burning appliance which is using up the oxygen then you have to make extra sure that fresh air enters the home. Lack of oxygen otherwise causes the appliance to burn the fuel incompletely and thereby to produce carbon monoxide fumes which are extremely poisonous.

In the kitchen, where cooking produces moisture, smells and dirt, there should always be adequate fresh air ventilation near the cooker. An extractor fan is probably most effective for reducing smells which otherwise tend to disperse around the house — but make sure, if you have a gas cooker, that there is enough oxygen coming in to feed the flames. If these are starved of oxygen, the unburned gas fills the room and could explode, demolishing your home as well as your insulation.

In most homes, however, quite enough air is supplied by air bricks and provided those are kept clear, you need not worry about stopping up draughts elsewhere. The thing to remember is that most houses are over-ventilated. Just use your common sense to prevent turning a room into a 'gas chamber' where there might be a danger of explosion or suffocation.

Once your house is well insulated and you have turned

your heating down accordingly, as much as a quarter of your heat loss will be through ventilation. Be sure to draughtproof wherever possible, leaving only the functional ventilation bricks open. You might think of fitting trickle ventilation (see page 26) to certain windows. The air supply can then be controlled to suit outside wind speeds without turning small leaks into huge ones.

The controllable devices also allow you to have gentle ventilation in operation while the house is empty, which is probably the best time to dry out moisture created by domestic use. You can then confidently proceed to draughtproof all uncontrollable leakage and reduce your energy wastage to the barest minimum.

4.
INSULATION — THE TEA COSY EFFECT

Once you have made yourself more comfortable and saved a good deal of money by draughtproofing, you can tackle the general matter of insulation. The easiest and most rewarding task to begin with is insulating the roof.

As much as a quarter of all the heat that escapes from your home goes through the roof. The combination of draughts, rushing in and pushing warm air upwards, and a badly insulated roof or loft, which allows the heat to disappear into the atmosphere, may in fact account for half the total heat loss. Loft insulation generally costs a good deal less than insulating other parts of the house (walls, floors and double glazing for windows) and it makes sense to tackle the roof at an early stage. On average, loft insulation pays for itself within three years. However, do not forget that once the loft has been insulated, the heat loss by conduction through walls and windows will be more intense.

LOFTS

In general the easiest and most popular way of insulating is to put a layer of insulating material on the floor of the roof space (where the cold water tank is). If you use the loft as a spare bedroom or study you have to insulate the underside of the roof itself. This is slightly more expensive and requires a bit more DIY skill than loft floor insulation but is nonetheless well worth doing.

The insulation has to be fixed permanently and satisfactorily. You cannot just bodge it up and hope it will last. (Though my own loft was lined for 15 years with a

piece of old carpet felt my sister and I found in a skip.
This is not what any expert would recommend, of course,
but I was very badly off at the time, it was free and it did
actually prevent any freeze-ups over those years.)

You must guard against fall-out from irritating fibres,
particularly if you use fibreglass. There may be a danger
of condensation forming because the moisture no longer
has anywhere to escape to, so be sure to leave enough
ventilation space between the tiles or slates. Unless you
are a dedicated or experienced DIYer it would probably
be best to get this sort of insulation done by a professional
builder. If you insist on doing it yourself, check all the roof
beams for rot or woodworm before covering them up and
forgetting about them. Take the precaution of treating
them against any such disasters in the future.

For homes with pitched roofs, the cheapest, easiest and
most effective method of insulation is to cover the loft
floor with one of the various materials specially produced
for the purpose. These include fibreglass, rockwool and
polystyrene granules. There are four basic kinds of roof
insulating materials.

Mat or quilt   These are rolls of glass fibre or spun mineral wool which you buy from DIY shops or hardware shops. The standard width is 40 cm (16 in) and this is about right to fit the normal distances between ceiling joists. If you need to, you can buy wider rolls from builders' merchants. For the most effective insulation you should use rolls of at least 7.5 cm (3 in), but they also come in thicknesses from 2.5 cm (1 in) (not nearly enough) to 10 cm (4 in) which is adequate. The thicker the roll, the more effective it will be and in Sweden, where winters are cold and long, 25.5 cm (10 in) is quite normal. Any extra expense is usually worth the return in savings. The cost of insulating an average, three bedroom semi-detached house with 10 cm (4 in) rolls should be recouped after about two years.

Glass fibre is a bit of a beast to install in the cramped and dusty conditions of a loft, but it will not take more than an afternoon or evening of discomfort. To cut down on the chance of irritation from mineral wool and glass fibre, wear gloves and a nose mask. Unwrap the rolls in the loft and work gently with them so that any loose fibres will not be blown about. When you have finished the job rinse your hands under cold water before washing to reduce possible irritation. Take the trouble to lay the mat snugly. Once it is laid, it should last as long as the house itself.

Loose fill   This is made from grains of cork or polystyrene or from pellets of mineral wool or glass fibre. The advantage of using these materials over glass fibre matting is that they fill up oddly shaped spaces more easily, for instance, around chimneys or between unevenly spaced joists. You should aim for 10 cm (4 in) of insulation. If this means the fill will cover the joists, nail raised strips of wood to the tops of the joists, so that you can identify them in case you need to get to the tank or pipes in the loft at a later date.

After pouring the grains into place they should be spread evenly about. You can use a home-made template

for this. The fibre pellets have to be tramped down a bit and will then be fairly resistant to draughts. When covering pipes and working at the eaves, lay down pieces of cardboard or building paper first. These can be bought in rolls. For the trap door, make a box frame, top it up with the fill and then cover it with plywood or hardboard.

Reflective aluminium foil   This is very cheap but not on its own sufficient insulation because it only cuts down losses in radiated heat. You staple the sheets to the joists or lay them slightly crumpled between them. A combination of both, using two sheets, is more effective. In the summer, the advantage of reflective insulation is that it keeps out heat from the sun, which often causes roof spaces to become painfully hot and muggy.

Foil, being very cheap and thin, makes excellent backing for other types of insulation. Some types of matting on the market use it as a backing sheet and this adds considerably to their insulating value.

Blown material Types of blown material (mineral or cellulose fibre) are most effective as insulation but expensive as you need a professional contractor to do the job. This may be the answer if you are elderly and qualify for a full council grant (see page 91). When shopping, look for good discounts on rolls of insulating fibre in builders' merchants and DIY shops. You are more likely to find bargains if you look in spring or summer.

Doing the work

Before you buy any material, take thorough and accurate measurements. Measure the distances between the joists, the lengths of the joists and the number of spaces between them. While you are about it, note the size of the water tank and check the lengths and sizes of the pipes. These have to be lagged after the loft floor has been insulated because the air is going to be considerably colder up there and freezing weather will lead to frozen pipes.

You will need a board or a couple of boards wide enough to span the joists. This will be your working platform — do not put your foot through gaps in the joists into the ceiling of the room below, as I once did, astonishing my daughter who was in bed. You will need a small saw and a large pair of scissors for cutting the rolls to size. They usually tear quite easily but there is not much elbow room in most lofts and you must make sure to get a tight fit.

Use a torch or, even better, an inspection lamp in a wire cage with a long extension lead. You can clip this to a beam or rafter so that it gives you a working light which is much better than a torch wedged precariously between bits of plank. You will also need a fairly long piece of wood for pushing the material into far corners.

Once the loft has been insulated, condensation may occur and cause damage to the timber unless you make sure there is adequate ventilation. If there is no ventilation in the loft space already (there probably is — check for chinks of daylight and for draughts) you will have to make holes in the eaves, but this is unlikely.

Extra roof space insulation can be provided by fixing

hardboard or aluminium-backed building paper to the rafters. This also helps to keep the loft space clean and dry. Use screws rather than nails so that you do not have to hammer the roof which might unsettle it.

While you are in the loft, check also for torn or frayed electric wiring. Wherever possible insulation should not cover wiring as this will make electrical work harder in the future.

Things to remember are:

- Use a secure pair of steps to get up into the loft, not one chair balanced on another.
- Where possible lay the insulation *over* pipes.
- Do not forget to insulate and draughtproof the trap door and make sure the seal is tight.
- Do not insulate under the tank. Leave a gap so that a little warmth can come up from downstairs to prevent it freezing up in bad weather.
- Do cover the top of the tank with a board and see that the ball cock is protected. That is often the part which freezes up first.

Lagging tanks and pipes

Once the loft has been insulated it is essential to insulate the tank and any piping which is still exposed. A burst pipe could bring your ceiling down and the loss of your water supply brings hideous inconvenience and expense, as many people discovered during the cold winter of 1986/7.

Tank

There may be enough material left over from your loft insulation to cover the tank. In this case just wrap the strips of mat around it and hold them in place with string or sticky tape. For the top, cut a piece of hardboard or plywood to size and stick on a couple of pieces of matting to make an effective insulated cover. Do not insulate underneath the tank, which cuts off the warmth rising up from downstairs.

If you have used loose fill and there are some bags left over, make a box around the tank and fill it with the stuff. The top will have to be like a tray to hold the insulation — make sure you do not get pieces of fibre in the tank and keep the water clean.

There are tank lagging kits available on the market but remember that to be really effective the insulation has to be at least 2.5 cm (1 in) thick or 5 cm (2 in) if you are using mineral wool. Such kits are quite cheap and relatively easy to fix, and make a fairly neat job of tank lagging.

Jackets made of polystyrene are convenient because they are easy to cut into, allowing the inlet, outlet and overflow pipes to get through. The kits, which contain four side sections and a top, come in many sizes, accommodating most sizes of tank. Alternatively you can buy sheets of polystyrene and cut them to size yourself using tape to fix them in place. These jackets are cheap to buy but if you are truly strapped for cash, you will find a blanket, an old duvet or even a sleeping bag to be effective.

Sometimes a U-shaped expansion pipe from the hot water cistern comes up to empty into the cold tank. If this is the case with yours, leave enough room when you cut a slot for it so that you can get at the valve should you need to. If this pipe ends above the tank, drill a hole in the insulation board below it and insert a plastic funnel. Hot water rarely comes out but if it does, you do not want it to ruin the insulation.

Hot water tank

An outlay of as little as £6-7 for a tank jacket could save you as much as £70 on the annual fuel bill. A well fitting tank jacket reduces heat loss from the tank by 75 per cent. It also enables you to turn your immersion heater thermostat down and to make more use of off-peak electricity. You must get a jacket which is the correct size for the tank and which is at least 7.5cm (3in) thick. If you already have a jacket on your tank, fit a new one over it.

These jackets come tightly rolled so fluff up the material to its full thickness before wrapping it round the cistern. They usually come in segments so work from the top downwards, make sure you fit the pieces evenly and leave no gaps. If there is an unavoidable gap, shove a rolled up piece of old blanket there before tightening the straps. Do not cover the top of an immersion heater or any taps or electric cables.

For slightly less cost you can make your own tank lagging by filling plastic rubbish bags with any surplus insulation matting from the loft. Use two bags for each piece so the irritating mineral fibres cannot escape. If you have any loose-fill material left you might box it in around the tank with hardboard or cardboard.

If you are thinking of replacing your existing tank, a factory insulated tank which has a built-in polyurethane layer costs only slightly more than an uninsulated tank. As an immediate measure, blankets or an old quilt tied around the tank will keep the heat from escaping until you have time to do a permanent job.

If, before lagging, you used the heat from your cistern in

the airing cupboard as a means of drying clothes and are worried about losing this convenience — do not be. The amount of heat lost from an unlagged tank is ridiculously high and when properly insulated, there will still be quite enough heat generated to air clothes. Remember that tank insulation is likely to have paid for itself within a month of its being fitted.

The cost of insulation for hot water tanks and pipes may be covered by a grant (see page 85).

Cold feed pipes

When lagging the pipes, from the cistern in the loft to the bathroom and hot water tank, remember that the insulation has to be at least 3 cm (1¼in) thick. As with the tank, you can use strips of left-over mineral wool matting. Wind them around the pipes in a spiral, overlapping each pipe and fix in place with tape. More easy and quite cheap are the lengths of polyurethane foam tubing you can buy. These come in several sizes to fit the standard sizes of pipe. They are split down one side so are easy to put on and, because they spring closed, just a few places will need taping, for instance at sharp bends in the piping.

Hot water pipes

When you turn on your hot taps, you probably find you have to run off quite a bit of water before it comes out hot. This is because the water in the pipe which runs from the tank to the tap has been allowed to cool. When you consider the whole network of pipes running from the hot water cistern and between the boiler and the tank, it amounts to a large surface area. Lagging these pipes stops the heat escaping and gives you more hot water. Again, the foam tubing is ideal for this job but strips of any insulating fabric will do. Remember to overlap so as to get a double thickness and pay special attention to where the pipes are hottest (from the boiler to the tank) and where they pass through the coldest places (along outside walls). Try the hot tap afterwards and you will get piping hot water coming through instantly.

If you are using felt bandage for lagging, you should overlap as you go, because the felt is not thick enough to give sufficient insulation on its own. If your pipes, like mine, have been fixed so close to the wall that you cannot get the tubing right round them, you have to tape them all the way along. For a thorough job it would probably be more sensible to build a wooden box round the pipes and fill that with insulating material.

WALLS

It is currently estimated that 20-35 per cent of the total heat loss from an average house is through the walls. This is a huge amount. Once you have stopped up the draughts and insulated the loft, the walls then account for most of your heat loss and energy wastage. Insulation will cut this by up to 66 per cent. However, the cost of wall insulation is much higher than for other basic home insulation techniques and it must be fitted professionally (although the proficient DIY enthusiast could cope with some methods of interior solid wall insulation).

Cavity walls

Most houses built in the second half of this century have cavity walls. This means that the outside walls of the house are actually two walls, an outer and an inner wall with a gap of 5 cm (2 in) of air between them. Cavity walls built since 1945 are constructed with insulation material in the gap and are fairly efficient at keeping the heat in. Older ones have only air between the two leaves and though they retain heat slightly more than solid walls, there is not much in it.

It is much easier and cheaper to insulate cavity than solid walls, but neither is really cheap. Your home will nevertheless be a good deal more comfortable and the heating bills drastically reduced if you can afford to have the insulating done.

Cavity wall insulation is not a DIY job. It must be done by an approved contractor using either foam, mineral wool or polystyrene beads. Get advice from the trade association. Not all cavities can be insulated and certain types of fill may be unsuited to your home.

Cavity wall insulation is well worth while as a home improvement and will raise the value of the property. By cutting the fuel bills it starts paying for itself immediately, saving on average £100 a year with a total payback period of around four years. As an idea of the costs you may expect, an 'average' terraced house costs £300 if filled with foam, £400 with polystyrene; a semi-detached home £400 for foam and £500 for polystyrene; a bungalow £450 for foam and £550 for polystyrene and a detached house £500 plus for foam and £600 plus for polystyrene depending on size and shape.

It is very important to use a contractor approved by one of the trade associations so that you know the work will be done properly and any problems promptly rectified. There are a number of 'cowboy' firms around with all sorts of tempting deals, but do not be persuaded. This is too much money to be fooling around with.

HOWDY, MA'AM, WE'VE COME ABOUT YOUR CAVITIES

Solid walls

Pre-war houses have solid walls with no gap, which are usually 23 cm (9 in) thick. This is not thick enough to keep heat in or to act as a storage heater. You can get external wall insulation — the External Wall Insulation Association will supply a list of its members. The choice of finishes ranges from rendering, resin coating and cladding boards to tiles, slates, pebble dash and many others. If your walls are old and in bad shape, you will not only be saving energy by having external insulation put up, but also improving your home's appearance.

External insulation can cost up to £3,000 and is obviously a major step, for which you may also need to get planning permission. Outside wall insulation is not a perfect solution, since it is very expensive and involves a lot of altering of doors, window sills, guttering and so on, which changes the appearance of the house.

Internal walls

In many ways this is a more satisfactory way of insulating if you can do it. It increases the comfort of your home, reduces the heating bills and leaves you with a well prepared surface for paint or paper. You will, however, make the room quite a bit smaller and will also have to do a lot of work altering window and door frames, moving electric points and replastering.

Since this is a fairly major job, you could do it as a first step when you are about to redecorate anyway. The easiest method is to use thermal boards, made up of plasterboard with an insulating backing of expanded polystyrene or urethane foam. If you feel competent at DIY put the insulation up yourself (the boards should be ordered from builders' merchants) otherwise get a professional to do it.

It is a lengthy process and likely to disrupt the household. You may have to do quite a lot of preparation beforehand if the brickwork is uneven or existing plaster is in bad condition.

Plastering must be done by a professional. Do not forget

to remove all door and window mouldings beforehand and when removing electrical fittings, make sure that the power is switched off at the mains. You may also have to renew the skirting boards.

Another method is to fix a framework of timber battens to the wall and fill between them with insulation such as mineral wool. These are covered with polythene sheets as a barrier against damp and finished off by fixing plasterboard or a decorative wallboard. Again, skirting boards, door and window mouldings and electrical fittings have to be removed beforehand. Cracks where boards meet can be filled with plaster or plasterboard joint tape.

The average cost of internal wall insulation is £10 to £15 per square metre. Doing the work yourself, could amount to around £800 for an average three bedroom house. Getting a contractor in, it could cost as much as £1,200. Either way, if you can afford it, and if you can bear the disruption, wall insulation will eventually pay for itself.

Quick and basic wall insulation

To reflect the heat from radiators back into the room, radiator wall panels are available which have a layer of aluminium. There is also a new type of wallpaper incorporating a layer of aluminium foil to put behind radiators. This is inexpensive, so it is worth doing.

There are other simple ways of reducing heat loss through walls and thereby making rooms cosier in the winter. If you live in a rented flat or, for any other reason, you are not prepared to do an involved insulation job, you should certainly consider some of the following.

Where there are two outside walls in a room, you will be accustomed to the way a single heating appliance pushes warmth out only as fast as the walls draw it away. Hanging a large rug or heavy curtain along a big area of blank wall has an immediately warming effect. Velvet is a good material for this, and if it is lined, so much the better.

Framed pictures and large expanses of shelving closely

filled with books would not be something recommended by the experts. But I have a largish library of books lining the walls of my living room and have found that they do quite substantially help to keep the cold out and the heat in. Since paper is a bad conductor of heat the warmth is not led out through the books.

Rolls of polystyrene of the type which self-extinguish in case of fire can be bought to stick on to walls. The thicker the better, of course. Polystyrene damages easily so it will not last long but should in any case be covered with wallpaper or a textured wallcovering which helps to protect it.

Wall hangings and textured wallcoverings also help keep the warmth in. Large patchwork quilts can turn your home into an insulated padded cell. Thick, dark cork is an excellent insulator — use it as an enormous pinboard or to cover a whole wall.

Wood insulates well and can be used, for instance, in the form of matchboarding (tongue and groove). It can be laid horizontally, vertically or diagonally. The boards are fixed to battens on the wall or ceiling and can be sealed or painted. Thick wallpaper, backed fabrics, wood panelling, cork, flock wallpapers, hessian, felt and so on are all helpful.

If your home still suffers from condensation, after you have already increased the ventilation and provided constant background heat, any of the above warm, textured surfaces may help.

FLOORS

An average house might lose 15 per cent of its heat through the floors. If you have draughtproofed between floorboards and at the skirtings, this heat loss will already have been reduced. Carpeting or other floor coverings, such as lino or cork, add to the cure and a good felt or rubber underlay achieves a massive improvement — especially with solid floors, concrete laid on hardcore or quarry tiles for instance. Never underestimate the power of carpet underlay and never skimp on it.

On timber floors, where it is possible to get under the boards, insulation can be laid beneath. You can use the same type as for loft insulation but ventilation is vital so do not block off any air bricks. This job is probably not worth your while unless you are pulling up the floorboards anyway to replace them or to treat rot or worm below. Unless you are particularly competent yourself you must get a contractor for this work.

A 'floating floor' can be fixed over existing concrete. This consists of a layer of hard expanded polystyrene slabs covered first with polythene sheet (as a vapour check) followed by two layers of hardboard constituting the new floor. The skirting boards must be taken out and replaced at the end of the operation and you have to take about 2 cm (¾in) off the bottom of any doors.

If you are lifting the floorboards, you may be able to insert blanket insulation in a hammock of netting fixed to the underside of the joists. You need at least a 2.5 cm (1 in) gap between the top of the insulation and the underside of the floorboards. Lag any pipes you discover under there and check all the woodwork for rot and worm. Treat it anyway, as insurance for the future.

Damp in a timber floor, a basement or cellar which is basically well built and in good condition may be cured if you clear away any earth and old leaves which have blocked up the air bricks in the outside walls. You may have to put in new air bricks to ventilate the underfloor area. A wooden floor in bad condition, however, is best removed and replaced by concrete or asphalt incorporating a damp proof membrane.

CEILINGS

Ceiling tiles or panels are an effective way of reducing heat loss and cheap and easy to fix. They also help reduce noises from upstairs. Many different kinds are available. Fix them by covering the whole tile with adhesive. Do not put the glue on in blobs. This can be a fire hazard because the air between the blobs can encourage flames.

As you can see, the level of insulation and also the cost can vary enormously. At one end of the scale you have cheap and effective draughtproofing and roof insulation with possibly a grant to help you; at the other cavity wall or solid wall insulation which is a major project and very expensive. The best solution is to do what you can afford and plan to do more as soon as possible. In the long run, all such insulation will cut heat losses and pay for itself — though in some cases that may take ten or twenty years.

5.
WINDOWS

Glass forms hardly any barrier at all to heat loss: the inside of the glass is as cold as the outside and any air coming into contact with it is immediately cooled. If you stand near a window on a cold day you feel this coldness quite a few inches away. As it cools the air drops, making a downdraught around your feet which can be very uncomfortable. Any moisture in the air caused by cooking, washing or even breathing turns into condensation on the window, which forms puddles and ice in sub-zero temperatures. If it happens all the time the window frames will rot.

It is estimated that single pane windows are responsible for 10-30 per cent of the heat lost from your home. The obvious answer would seem to be double glazing, but think again. Professional double glazing is expensive and involves a lot of work and mess. A full-blown professional job pays for itself in terms of energy savings' only after 30 or 40 years, in spite of what advertisements claim. These usually emphasise the value added to your house, but the value certainly will not be more than it costs you to do the double glazing anyway.

Unless you are using the 'double-sided-tape-and-polythene-sheet' system, you can be pretty sure it will not be worthwhile double glazing the whole house professionally.

In the sixties, when fuel was plentiful and cheap, architects and builders tended to forget about heat conservation. On housing estates it was fashionable to build houses with picture windows (although they usually faced each other so there was not much 'picture' involved). These large windows were usually single-glazed and the occupants often could not afford enough central heating to prevent some of the worst condensation. The same thing happened with many of the concrete, high-rise blocks of flats built at around the same time. Insulation was minimal, glazing single and only later, when fuel became expensive, did it become apparent what problems these spacious windows created.

Double glazing insulates because the pocket of air between the two panes is isolated — it neither mixes with the air inside nor outside. The ideal width for this air space is about 2 cm (1 in). At widths less than this the heat losses are greater, while if the gap is wider the heat losses are broadly the same. If you have decided to install double glazing to reduce noise from outside, the gap between panes should be much wider, about 15 cm (6 in) and in this case, heat savings are reduced.

Although double glazing may reduce heat loss through windows by up to half, unless it is done very cheaply (usually by yourself) it is almost certainly not cost

effective for standard, smallish windows. Where there is a
particularly large window or a whole-wall picture window,
or in rooms which are well heated every day, such as the
living room, the discomfort and chilly conditions of that
room in the winter probably justify a good double glazing
job. If you are thinking of replacing any window frames or
turning a window into a French window, it would be
foolish not to double glaze while you are about it since you
are paying so much for the job anyway.

PROFESSIONAL AND SKILLED DIY

Double glazed replacement windows　This is the
Rolls Royce of double glazing. Replacement windows are
the soundest but the most expensive. They are factory
made to replace existing windows and come hermetically
sealed, either with the two panes of glass fused together at
the edges or with a sealed metal or plastic spacer all the
way round. In both kinds, the air inside is completely
encased and there is therefore little danger of
condensation reducing the insulation value. Only two
surfaces (outside and inside) will need cleaning.

This type of window is by far the best looking, because
to all intents and purposes it constitutes a single frame
and looks like a single pane of glass. The work must,
however, be done by skilled people and with care because
a good fit is absolutely essential.

When looking for a supplier, make sure the company is
a member of the Glass and Glazing Federation and that
there is a guarantee to cover the eventuality of a poor seal
causing condensation or any other wrong. For instance, it
has been known for a company to go bankrupt in the
middle of a job, so you want to be insured in case this
happens, or at least guaranteed that the company pays
somebody else to finish the job.

The Federation operates a Code of Ethical Practice,
drawn up with the Office of Fair Trading to ensure that
customers get a fair deal and proper after-sales service if
anything goes wrong or needs to be put right. It is

probably in your interests to deal only with firms belonging to the Federation.

Secondary sashes With secondary sashes the existing frames and window panes are left in place and a new vertically or horizontally sliding sash in aluminium or plastic is fitted to the inside of the frame. Double glazing is effected by the gap between the old and new panes.

These are more common than replacement windows because they are considerably cheaper to fit. If you install them yourself, they are cheaper still. Some firms insist on doing the fitting themselves to ensure airtightness but as the sliding sashes use brush contact seals, complete airtightness is a fairly vain hope. Make sure that the frame is sturdy enough to take the added weight of an extra pane of glass.

Cleaning is, of course, doubled and condensation almost bound to occur because moisture will get through. There may also be a danger from vertical sliders with no counterweight or spring that you end up with sorely bashed fingers, especially if you have to lean over a sink or table to reach the window.

Secondary windows Like the secondary sashes, these are added to existing windows but open inwards instead of sliding. They also open and close independently and need extra cleaning. The gap between the panes is likely to be larger than with other types and manufacturers will stress the advantages in increased noise reduction to play down the loss of insulation efficiency. If you are an experienced DIYer, kits of secondary glazing systems may ease into their frames like butter in your capable hands. Kits can be bought to fit standard sizes of window and some firms cut frames to your specific needs and fix the glazing. You just have to fit them.

Hermetically sealed units   These are replacement panes, not complete replacement windows. You can order factory-made units from a glass or builders' merchant which are tailor made to the size you want. The hermetic seal gives a very good protection against condensation between the panes but is easily damaged before fixing and needs careful handling. If condensation does occur, the seal has been damaged.

This is a perfectly sound way of solving heat loss problems and is less expensive than replacement windows. To fit these yourself requires a high degree of skill and care, not to mention confidence, so do not undertake it lightly. You could spend a lot of money on the unit and lose it on inefficient fitting.

Make sure the existing frame and hinges can take the weight of a second pane of glass and choose a firm which gives a good guarantee (about ten years is reasonable). Breakages are expensive so add this to your house insurance. A new pane can be fitted to an existing pane so that it opens and closes with the original window.

Secondary sashes fitted to the outside These are quite rare but if you need or want secondary glazing fitted outside existing windows, it is available. Secondary frames have to be made strong enough to resist wind and rain while still being able to open and close and not look too awful. As it is so much easier to put secondary glazing on the inside, putting it outside seems financially and practically illogical. The likelihood is that it will cause severe condensation, too.

Triple glazing Tripe glazing uses three panes of glass, each separated from the other by 2.5cm (1in). If you use glass for them it is highly expensive, takes up a lot of space and probably is not worth the time and money. But a DIY job using plastic sheets instead of glass, and separate frames, will be cheaper and probably as effective as professional double glazing.

General points to remember
1. A sealed unit of two panes will be expensive to replace if it gets broken. Where there is any danger of this, insure against it. But apart from the money, who knows how long it will take to get your new pane?
2. If you are thinking of DIY as opposed to professional fitting, remember that if anything goes wrong (and it can be a tricky job) the firm will not take responsibility. My feeling is that having decided to install a costly system, it is worth going the whole hog by making sure it is the best of its kind and professionally fitted, even if it costs a bit more. Only do it yourself if you are getting the cheapest systems.
3. Some systems are available with 'low emissivity' glass where a special coating on the glass reflects heat back into your room. This further reduces heat loss quite substantially.
4. Most double glazing comes in either aluminium, timber or PVC which is a rigid, weather resistant plastic. Aluminium, though popular, is not

necessarily appropriate. In older homes it looks downright out of place and you would be better off with timber. Modern timber treatments mean that wooden frames have a long life provided they have been cured properly. You will have to balance up appearance against cost.

Here is a short checklist to help you decide where and what kind of double glazing you might think it worth installing:

1. Double glazing is most effective in rooms heated to high temperatures for long periods, for instance in the living room.
2. Most professional systems offer a wide choice, yet there will rarely be much difference in effectiveness. Shop around and get quotes from three or four suppliers. There are marked differences in price.
3. Look at the construction and spacing of the glazing. Very large gaps are only useful for sound reduction and sealed units will be resistant to condensation.
4. Never be bullied into making a quick decision, and do not sign anything until you have properly discussed your needs with the rest of the family.
5. Consider the system from the point of view of cleaning and maintenance. There are huge variations and you might as well get something convenient. How easily can the windows be opened and closed, for instance?
6. If you are replacing a window anyway, compare the cost of a single glazed one with a double glazed one. You may feel justified in going for the double glazing.

CHEAP DIY WINDOW INSULATION

More people are beginning to discover that effective double glazing can be done easily and cheaply, if only as a winter measure, with sheets of polythene and a roll of double sided sticky tape. This method is, of course, only intended to last for one season and is not anything like as efficient as replacement windows or the more elaborate secondary windows. But it will enable you to double glaze your whole house for only a few pounds.

You can choose between flexible sheets of plastic and the thinner sheets of self-adhesive plastic film, which only last for one season. The thicker sheets can be taken down in the summer, stored for the duration and used again. The four most common methods are all described in full below.

Plastic sheets   Measure the windows carefully. For large sized windows you may need to order the plastic. You can use double-sided adhesive tape but there are fixing materials on the market specifically designed for flexible plastic such as plastic edging strips, Velcro tape or magnetic tape. You should use 12mm ($\frac{1}{2}$in) wide tape.

Wash the window frames first and allow them to dry out completely. Then stick the tape around the edge of the frame, leaving the backing tape in place. Measure the inside of the window frame and add 5mm ($\frac{1}{4}$in) to allow for the tape at the top of the frame and stick the top of the sheet in place, stretching it taut. Remove the rest of the backing tape, holding the sheet by the corners at the bottom, pull it taut and position it. Then press it into place, getting as tight a fit as you can. Two pairs of hands might make this job easier. Trim the plastic so it reaches the edge of the tape, using a straight edge (a long metal ruler or straight stick) and a very sharp knife. Take care not to score the paintwork underneath.

Cling film   Cling film sticks to any surface that is not greasy so use some washing-up liquid or decorators' detergent with warm water to clean and de-grease the window frame. When the frame is truly dry, stick the corner of a roll of cling film to the top. Using your little fingers as rollers and your thumbs and forefingers to hold the corners of the unrolled film, press a couple of inches into place around the top of the frame. Then use your thumbs to press out any air bubbles. When the entire width of the film has got a good grip, gently unfurl the roll pressing it against the frame as you go.

Keep a slight tension so you get a good initial fit. When you get to the bottom of the frame cut the roll away with a razor blade. The film can then be refitted so as to remove any crinkles and to get a smooth, taut sheet. Start at one corner, pick a short distance of the film away from the frame, stretch it tight and reseal it over the paintwork. Repeat this until you have covered the whole frame. Using a hair dryer on the edges will gently tighten the hold. The important thing is to clean the window frames first.

Rigid plastic   There are several DIY kits which use glass or rigid plastic and come with edging strip or, for plastic, magnetic strip. With a plastic and magnetic strip kit there is an adhesive magnetic strip which you fit to the window frame and a magnetic strip which is fitted to the secondary glazing. When the job is finished the glazing can be easily positioned and removed when you wish. Instructions come with these kits but you will also need a small hacksaw for cutting the strip and a sharp knife with

a blade suitable for cutting the plastic. Remember to thoroughly wash the window frames and let them dry before applying the adhesive strip.

Plastic or glass and edging strip   The kit should include glass or plastic panel, edging strip and fasteners. Get the plastic or glass cut for you allowing 1 cm (½in) extra for each edge. Decide whether you want to fit it to the window so that it opens, or to the window recess.

The edging strip should be pressed around the edge of the glass starting from the middle of one side. Mitre the corners by cutting a V shape in the strip where two ends meet. (Sometimes a mitre block is supplied with the kit.) Hold the panel in position or get someone to do it for you and mark the edges for the fasteners, two by each corner at the top and bottom. Then loosely screw in the fasteners. Position the glazing and tighten up the fasteners. Now the panel will be fixed in place and you can fit the rest of the fasteners.

WHICH WINDOWS?

It is rarely worth double glazing the whole house, so be selective about the windows you double glaze. Most living rooms, which are heated to a fairly high temperature all day, benefit from double glazing — especially if the windows are large or there are enormous patio doors. Double glazing in this case makes more of the room comfortable to sit in. It is interesting to watch people steer clear of the window area of well heated rooms which have single glazing because of the chill.

There is no real alternative to a professional job on such major windows, but the benefits are guaranteed. You will be able to turn down your heating and no longer waste a lot of energy counteracting the 'negative radiation' caused by large surface areas of cold glass. If you have a thermostat in your living room, controlling the whole home heating system, it is often set needlessly high just to cope with the demands of the living room.

If your home boasts a large bay window, the areas of wall in between individual windows will, altogether, lose more heat than a similar area of flat wall. Bay windows are easy to insulate yourself by using one of the DIY methods because the windows are probaby of a manageable size. Where there are several sashes, double glaze a couple and leave the rest for occasional ventilation. Alternatively you could fit insulating shutters (page 68) to fill the whole bay. These are of most use in the evening when the atmosphere is coldest.

DOUBLE GLAZING AND CONDENSATION

Double glazing reduces condensation on windows but not the humidity in the air which causes it. The water droplets will probably try to settle elsewhere — on a cold wall, for instance. Make sure a window can be opened every now and then, especially in kitchens and bathrooms where steam from cooking, washing, bathing and so on can cause quite horrific condensation problems.

Whenever people are gathered together in a confined space their breath produces a lot of moisture and therefore condensation. You can see this on the car windscreen when two or three people are inside on a cold rainy day, especially if the fan and heater are turned off. A hermetically sealed double glazing system will not attract any condensation, but no other double glazing is completely condensation free. You must be able to open the inner sashes of secondary glazing in order to remove any water and you will continue to get condensation on the metal frames of a double glazing system, especially if the sections are wide. A weak solution of bleach temporarily solves mould problems.

If a pane is to be permanently closed, ventilation holes of about 5mm ($\frac{1}{4}$in) should be drilled at the bottom of each main frame, leading to the outside. This alleviates condensation. Keep the holes plugged with glass wool to keep out the moths and dirt.

OTHER WAYS OF INSULATING WINDOWS

Shutters

Shutters have been used on windows in homes for
centuries and for sound practical reasons — they act like
double glazing but, being opaque, effectively wall in the
heat. It is a great pity that houses are no longer built with
shutters or at least with allowance for them. Often in
modern flats the windows are built right up to the side of
the wall so that there is no room to pull a curtain right
back, let alone for a shutter.

People sometimes buy shutters for their decorative
value without thinking of them as extra insulation. Mass-
produced louvre doors are especially popular but they do
not provide an effective insulation barrier. However,
insulation shutters for windows can be made at a fraction
of the cost of double glazing and to greater effect. You are
unlikely to want to use them during the day (though I
know people living in a large Georgian house who do keep
the lower shutters closed during very cold spells, and there
is still enough light coming through the top to see by) but
during the evening and at night when the air is coldest
shutters are an efficient form of insulation.

You can make your own insulating shutters out of
boards of insulating material, such as expanded hard
polystyrene rather than the traditional heavy solid wood,
fitted into a light timber frame (plywood is probably best).
This can be painted or covered with fabric or wallpaper to
match the rest of the room.

It is important to take accurate measurements. A good
fit in the window frame is necessary to prevent air
circulating behind the shutters. You want to trap the air
to give added insulation value. Construction of insulation
shutters requires home craftsmanship and adequate space,
but would be quite within the scope of the average DIYer.

Shutters should be fitted to the window frame with
strong hinges or lift-in panels. To cut down the risk of fire,
they may also be covered with fireproof building board
which makes them heavier, or you could use a self-
extinguishing material inside.

Curtains

A well fitted curtain can provide as good insulation as a
double glazed window. As with shutters, you do not want
to draw the curtains across a window during daylight, but
at night they are marvellous insulators, particularly if
they are made of heavy material and lined. For maximum
effect, curtains should be fitted inside the window opening
with the curtain ends stopping on the sill to prevent down
draughts. If this is not possible, or does not look attractive,
you can attach a board or box pelmet over the rail,
covering the gap between the rail and the wall. This
creates an efficient barrier to cold air and prevents it
pouring down through the curtains onto the floor and out
into the room around your feet.

Alternatively, ceiling-to-floor and wall-to-wall curtains,
which cover the whole wall when drawn, are dramatic to
look at and effective as insulation. They do not just stop
warm air escaping through the window but help to prevent
it being conducted through the whole wall. You need
heavy material such as velvet or wool, which is not cheap
but it will be a good deal cheaper than double glazing.

SAFETY

When planning double glazing remember to think what you are going to do in case of fire. If you and your family ever have to make a quick escape and all your windows have fixed PVC or glass double glazing, you will have to bash your way through. This will not only be difficult but also dangerous. Take care to have at least a few windows strategically placed which can be opened easily in an emergency.

6.
USING FUELS WISELY

Fuels are precious and we are too inclined to take them for granted. If we are to conserve them and try to make them last as long as possible, we must learn to use them in unwasteful ways. You can do this without having to be uncomfortable at home, just by being practical, sensible and thoughtful.

Central heating arrived on the domestic scene at a time when fuels seemed to be everlasting and were very cheap. Costs of natural fuels have gone up wildly and will increase in leaps and bounds now that we know these fuels are finite. I can remember having tussles with my husband about the living room thermostat; he would turn it up to 21°C (70°F) every time he walked past it, and I

YES, IT'S PURE COAL

would turn it down to 18°C (65°F) every time I went past.
Now that the house is insulated, I keep it at a constant
12°C (55°F) which we find satisfactory both in winter and
summer, except on very cold days when I boost it to 15°C
(60°F) and light the log fire.

In large, air-conditioned offices people walk around in
shirtsleeves in cold weather as though it were high
summer and we mistakenly expect we should be able to do
the same at home. But there is nothing wrong with woolly
sweaters and it is unnecessary, if not unhealthy, to keep
the home at a temperature of a tropical clime — even if
you can afford to! There is also a wonderful choice of
tracksuits, sweaters, leg warmers and winter boots
available on the market to keep us warm.

Many people are inclined to turn their heating up to
maximum the moment autumn officially arrives, leaving
themselves unprepared for the really cold weather which
does not hit until December or January. Very often
Britain has an Indian summer in September or October
when the evenings are a little chilly but the days are
bright and comparatively warm. It is foolish to overheat at
this stage and leave no margin for boosting the heat when
the weather really turns cold. To this day, in the north of
England and in Scotland, most people would not dream of
heating any room that was not actually being used at that
moment and the living room fire is often not lit until the
evening.

RUNNING COSTS

Electricity

Electricity is sold by the unit. One unit is consumed by
using electricity at the rate of one kw (1,000 watts) for one
hour. For example, a 100w light bulb uses one unit when it
burns for 10 hours, a 250w appliance uses one unit in four
hours and a 1kw fire uses one unit for every hour of use.
The following table lists some of the most common
household appliances and shows how much electricity you
can expect to get out of them for one unit.

What you get for one unit

100 watt light bulb	10 hours
60 watt reading lamp	17 hours or more
1 kw infra red heater	1 hour
2 kw convector heater	½ hour
2 kw storage radiator	Around 2,400 units per heating season (32 weeks) using low cost electricity
Warm air central heating	Uses mainly lower-cost night-rate electricity. Consumption can vary but the average yearly consumption is about 1,800 units
250 w towel rail	4 hours
Hot water heating	85 units will heat up the cylinder for a family of four (if the tank is lagged)
Cooker	3 family meals
Kettle	12 pints
Vacuum cleaner	2-4 hours
Refrigerator	1 day
Spindryer	4 hours
Tumble dryer	½ hour (a very expensive piece of equipment to run)
Iron	2 hours or more
Extractor fan	15 hours

Cooker hood	10 hours
Instant water heater	3 gallons
Electric underblanket	Over a week
Electric overblanket	2 full nights
Automatic washing machine	9 units for average family weekly wash
Twin tub	12 units for ditto
Shower	One shower a day for a week equals 10 units
Colour TV	7 hours
Stereo	8-10 hours
Tape recorder	24 hours or more

Off peak electricity   Economy 7 supplies electricity at two different rates. You pay ordinary rate for electricity used between 7am and 11pm and a cheaper night rate between 11pm and 7am. Off-peak electricity can be used for storage radiators, underfloor heating and other forms of electric heating designed to charge up at night. It is also useful for heating water in a well-lagged tank, cooking stews, casseroles and so on during the night on a timed cooker and for laundry or dishwashing, if your machines are quiet enough to be used at night.

Your local electricity board showroom should be able to advise if Economy 7 would be worth having in your home. They may send leaflets about this scheme with the quarterly bill. It is usually impossible to get through to them on the phone, but persevere, or send the Freepost form back to them.

Electric cooker   An electric cooker, on average, cooks one person's daily meals for one unit of electricity. If you are going to bake, try to make full use of the oven space.

Cook two or three dishes at the same time, eat one and
cool and freeze the others. Fill in empty spaces with baked
potatoes. If you have a cooker with two ovens, try to fit
everything into one, instead of using both unnecessarily.

Allot a baking day and cook all your bread, cakes,
biscuits, pastry and so on together. Cakes, biscuits and
bread freeze very well and will keep in airtight tins for
several months. For some dishes, such as casseroles and
joints, you can turn the oven off about quarter of an hour
before removing from the oven.

Never use the oven to try and heat the kitchen or to air
clothes. It is a terribly inefficient and wasteful way of
keeping warm. The oven is insulated and thermostatically
controlled. It does not consume unnecessary electricity
when used for what it was intended, which is cooking.

75

The grill uses as much electricity as the oven but as it is used only for short periods, it is often more economical for heating a small amount of food. Some grills have controls to use only half the surface area so that there is no wasted heat when cooking small quantities. For making toast or toasting crumpets, use a toaster as it is more economical.

Boiling rings are the most used parts of the cooker. They are fast and easily controlled so switch them on when you start cooking, not before, and switch off when you have finished. Do not leave them lingering on at cool.

Get a cooker with dual rings which can be set to heat up only at the centre for small pans, without wasting electricity on the outside. Always use pans with lids — it cuts down cooking time and does not cause nearly as much condensation. Cook as many different vegetables as you like in one pan — you can wrap them separately in foil. A pressure cooker also saves time, fuel and nutrients when cooking.

Microwave oven   These cookers use less electricity than conventional ovens since they require less fuel to activate the microwaves and the cooking time is shorter into the bargain.

Lighting   Fluorescent lighting uses less electricity than filament lighting and gives up to four times as much light. Fluorescents are available in perfectly acceptable 'warm' colours now and also in the form of much smaller tubes. If used in the kitchen, under the cupboards with a baffle to screen the actual tube from your eyes, they can be efficient, good looking and unwasteful.

With filament lighting there are many energy saving practices you can adopt. Switch off lights you are not using and use lower wattage bulbs on stairs, hallways and passages, so long as they give enough light for safety. In living rooms use several low wattage lamps rather than one high watt bulb from the ceiling. This gives you more flexibility. It may also be worthwhile installing dimmer switches. These are no harder on the bulbs but can save on electricity, particularly if you are using spot bulbs.

Washing machines   Use one of the powder or liquid 'cold water' detergents so you do not have to heat the water up so much. Britain is one of the few countries where people still insist on a hot wash. With modern detergent formulas, this is rarely necessary except perhaps for white cotton garments or extremely dirty overalls. America, Japan and the rest of Europe, all have cold fill machines and use cold water washes. This saves a lot of fuel.

Gas
Make sure you are on the right tariff for the amount of gas you use. If you use a pre-payment meter and a lot of gas, you can save considerably by changing to a credit meter. Ask at your local gas showroom.

Solid fuel
Open fires   Use the poker gently and sparingly — a long thin poker, is best. Keep the grate well filled and regulate burning by using the air control. This helps maintain a low burning rate without the fire dying out. Fit a throat restrictor in the flue immediately above the fire if the fire burns too merrily. It will also reduce cold draughts. Ask your local Solid Fuel Advisory Bureau or local builders' merchants.

   If you have a back boiler, adjust the boiler damper to medium position and regulate burning with the air control. Slow and steady is the rule, because it is much less wasteful than sudden boosts. Keep the boiler surfaces and flue clear of soot and ash by sweeping them once a fortnight, otherwise the heat getting to the water will be reduced.

Stove   The stove must be properly sealed into the fireplace or it may lose warmth from the room up the chimney. See that the fire door and ashpit cover fit

AT LEAST THE GARDEN'S WARM...

snugly. Leaks around these doors certainly waste fuel and make it difficult to control the burning rate. Any broken glass or mica in the firedoor should be replaced quickly.

Keep the firebox well filled and regulate the burning rate by air control. Run the appliance steadily, not erratically which is wasteful and bad for the stove. Keep your stove alight all the time if you can. It is more economical to keep the chill off rooms permanently than to have to heat the room up from cold every morning. It is also more comfortable and helps keep condensation at bay. Modern solid fuel kitchen cookers, boilers and many room heaters have thermostats which control the burning rate of the appliance.

CENTRAL HEATING

Central heating allows you to heat all or most of your home fairly uniformly. The fuel used may be gas, oil or solid which is generally burned in a boiler. The heat circulates around the house by means of radiators or warm air. Most types of modern central heating are generally cheaper to use than individual electric fires or bottled gas heaters.

If you go away for more than a couple of days, lower the thermostat setting on the central heating. In winter it is unwise to turn the heating off altogether in case there is a cold snap and your pipes burst.

Most central heating systems can cope with temperatures of 21°C (70°F) in living rooms, 18°C (65°F) in halls and bathrooms and 15°C (60°F) in bedrooms. But very few people need this amount of heat and you can save five per cent of your fuel for every degree centigrade you turn down your heating.

Reducing gas thermostats by 2°C (4°F) can lower gas consumption by up to 10 per cent. If the house is well insulated you may be able to lower this still more. Below are a few points to bear in mind:

- Close radiator valves and warm air grilles in rooms you are not using, and keep doors closed in warm rooms.
- Cure dripping taps by changing the washer, as even a slow drip can waste a lot of water and fuel. Only in very cold weather if you are afraid of the pipes freezing, leave a trickle until you manage to get the lagging done.
- If a room gets too warm do not open the windows. Turn the heating down.
- Draw the curtains at night, but not over radiators or you will prevent the heat from coming into the room.
- If radiators are fitted with thermostatic valves, set the valves at their lowest comfortable room temperature.
- If some radiators do not get warm, while others are very hot, consult your heating installer. He may be able to balance the system better.

Heating controls

A central heating system is only as efficient as the controls which regulate it, so do not economise at the expense of getting what is most appropriate. It is only worth paying for heating where and when you want it and at the temperature that you choose. There are a number of different types of controls for central heating systems which can achieve this.

Timers and programmers   The most basic system is one with a time switch or programmer which turns the boiler on and off at pre-set times. They can, for example, be set to warm the house up before you get up in the morning, to switch off during the day, warm up again before you get home and switch off at bed time.

Room thermostat   A room thermostat is usually a small circular dial placed on the wall in the living room or hall. The dial shows either temperatures (usually in centigrade) or numbers. A recommended temperature is about 21°C (70°F) but this is very high in my opinion. If you set your thermostat to the required temperature, the heating system is turned off automatically by the thermostat when it reaches that temperature and on again when it cools down. (Obviously in an insulated home, the room takes longer to cool, the thermostat longer to turn the heating on again and much heat will be saved.)

A day/night thermostat can be set so that it keeps the heating on very low, when you do not need it on full blast, instead of turning it off altogether as with a programmer. This helps to keep the chill off and ward off any condensation. The weakness of a central thermostat in one room is that the whole house is controlled from this point.

Zoned system   The more popular modern system is a zoned system with several thermostats so that different areas of the house are controlled separately. Such a system is not cheap because a completely independent switching arrangement has to be set up for each new thermostat. This is best done when the boiler and radiators are being installed.

One thing to watch out for is the preconceived notion that your heating engineer may have about how warm individual rooms ought to be. He may think in terms of 21°C (70°F) for the living room and 15°C (60°F) for bedrooms. In his eyes all rooms other than living rooms or kitchens are bedrooms, even if one is used as a workroom. If you want a workroom or a child's room at a higher temperature, you may have to bully him into it.

Radiator valves   Nearly all central heating radiators can be turned off by a valve situated at one of the bottom corners so you do not have to heat rooms unnecessarily.

Better still you can have each radiator fitted with a thermostatic valve which switches itself on and off, to keep the room at a different temperature from others. Thus bedrooms can be kept warm, but not during the day when not being used. It is obviously best to have them put in at the same time as the heating system, but you could install others on radiators in rooms less often used.

INDIVIDUAL HEATERS

Night storage heaters

Night storage heaters are filled with a special brick which is heated up overnight by electrical elements. The bricks gradually lose their heat to the room during the day. Because they use off-peak electricity (usually Economy 7) they are cheaper to run than other electric heaters mentioned below. Storage heaters provide useful background heat but they are often, especially the older type, cool or cold by the evening which is when you most want the heat. Those with good controls, however, allow you to regulate both the charging up over night and the flow of heat during the day.

For the elderly, for others who have no central heating or for those who do not want to use it and prefer to heat up just one room there are several types of heater available.

Electric heaters

These are convenient because they can be moved from one room to another and they are relatively cheap to buy. But they are the most expensive type of heating available as they run during the day. There are single bar electric fires of 1kw, also fan or blow heaters, convector heaters and oil filled radiators which are plugged into electric sockets. Most electric heaters use between 1kw and 3kw of electricity an hour. There is usually a small plate on the appliance to say what the kw rating is.

On electric radiant bar fires, it is best to keep the shiny surface behind the radiant bars clean and dust free to get the most heat from the fire. Fan heaters are easy to move around but they are not robust and the fan tends to jam if the appliance is not treated reverently.

Gas fires
Mains gas is at present one of the cheapest fuels available for heating. Gas fires are fairly common and are fitted to an outside wall or chimney breast as they need ventilation. Gas convector heaters usually have a 'balanced flue' which provides ventilation and they must be positioned on the outside wall.

Paraffin and similar heaters
These are mobile heaters which need to be filled up with fuel or have a space at the back for a refillable, portable fuel tank. Like gas fires, they need good ventilation to burn, especially as they produce a gallon of water for every gallon of fuel burned — not the best sort of heater for homes which suffer from condensation. They must be placed where they cannot be knocked over and should not be moved while they are lit.

Immersion heater
Generally it is best to switch an immersion heater on only when you need it, perhaps twice a day, rather than to keep it permanently on. On the other hand, do not keep switching it on and off all the time. The best thing would be to have it controlled by a time switch, which can be bought and fitted to the heater.

7.
GETTING FINANCIAL HELP

You may be able to get a grant for certain types of insulation in the home. In 1978 the government embarked on a ten-year plan to conserve energy by insulating the nation's roofs. In order to encourage this scheme they organised a system of grants for loft insulation. You can now get a grant for part of the cost of insulating your loft, if it has no insulation at present or if the existing insulation is 4 cm (1½in) thick or less.

GRANTS

Grants cover half the cost of insulation or £68, whichever is the smaller. The government has now extended this scheme so that up to 90 per cent of the cost can be claimed by the elderly. If you want to insulate, apply for the grant as soon as possible as most local councils have waiting lists and, because there is an upper limit to the grant, inflation is eating away at its value.

Grants may be made towards:

1. Insulating the loft (or other space if you have a flat roof).
2. Cutting a hatch or temporary hole in the ceiling (so that you can get in to do the work) and then making good afterwards.
3. Insulation of any cold water tank and pipes in the roof space.
4. Insulation for the hot water cistern (such as a tank jacket).

Grants are only given if your loft is uninsulated or if your existing insulation is below the 4 cm minimum thickness. It could even be worthwhile tearing out old or poor insulation in order to meet this requirement. The other regulation is that only approved materials should be used. Do not begin the work before you have been awarded the grant as you may not receive it after all.

If you think you might be eligible for a grant, get in touch with your local authority before starting work. They will probably send someone round to check out your home. If you are a pensioner, disabled, on a low income or receiving state benefits, you may be entitled to a special low cost or free service for draughtproofing your home or insulating the loft.

READING METERS

You can quite easily calculate your own fuel bills before the bill arrives.

Electricity

One unit of electricity on your meter equals about 5½p. If you want to check this, contact your local electricity showroom who should be able to tell you how much a unit costs in your area.

There are two kinds of meter, digital or dial. The digital meter is a line of figures. Copy down the line and in a week's or month's time copy it down again. Subtract the first reading from the second and you will see how many units you have used since the first reading. Off-peak meters usually have two lines of numbers, one for units used during off-peak periods ('low') and the other for the units used the rest of the time ('high').

Dial meters have a row of dials with hands which move in alternate directions from 0-9. To read the meter start with the left hand dial and write down the figures the hands point to. If the hand is between numbers, write the lower figure.

Gas

One therm of gas (about 100 cubic feet) costs about 38p. Check with your local gas board for precise and up-to-date figures. To find out how many therms you have used, write down the line of figures and subtract last week's reading from this week's. Ignore the red numbers. On a dial meter read only the bottom four dials.

PAYING BILLS

If you use coal, paraffin or bottled gas, you know exactly how much fuel you are using and therefore how much money you are spending at any one time. With gas and electricity, however, you cannot be sure until the end of the three months unless you know how to read your meter and calculate the cost of the number of units you have used. (See above for meter reading.)

There are a number of ways of paying the bills, other than as a lump sum at the end of every quarter.

1. You can pay an agreed amount weekly or monthly by standing order or direct debit from your bank. The amount is set by the gas or electricity board depending on how much they think your bill will be over the year. Usually they overestimate and owe you money most of the time. (My own bill came to £100 less than they had estimated for two years running and I got a huge rebate.) Normally they do not bother to pay you back but take it off the next cold quarter's bill. This is an expensive way of paying although it means you do not have to worry about the bills.
2. You can buy savings stamps at gas and electricity board showrooms towards your next bill.
3. You can arrange to pay as much as you like whenever you feel able towards your next bill.

Some of these schemes are particularly useful for pensioners, or people with young families.

KEEPING WARM ON A PENSION

For many pensioners the cost of heating can be a heavy burden in winter. This is specially true of people who are at home all day and are less active than they used to be. Fuel costs have risen steeply over the last five years and continue to rise. Many elderly people are afraid to use the heating for fear they will not be able to pay their bills. On top of that, with failing eyesight, less nimble fingers and unsteady legs, it is difficult for many elderly people to do the simple draughtproofing that helps keep the heat in. Nevertheless, many people find that by using only one room during the day they can make it warm and cosy and forget about the other rooms. Remember, the more insulation the smaller the bill.

There are also many easy and quick things that able-bodied, younger friends and relatives can help out with. The first is to draughtproof as described in chapter 3. This is a simple job and though most old people do not believe that it makes such a difference, their delight at the result is proof enough. In many areas around the country local insulation projects have been set up to help pensioners, disabled and low income households with insulation work, either free of charge or very cheaply. These 'Neighbourhood Energy Action' groups also offer practical and sensible advice.

Secondly, you can help older relatives or friends to make the most of the benefits and grants available to them for heating. About one million pensioners suffer unnecessary hardship because they do not claim what is their right. Older people often find it difficult to understand the forms and leaflets available to them and are often put off by a supercilious person on the other side of the counter when they go to the benefit office. Harassed and overworked civil servants do not always have patience with the hesitancies of the old. Relatives can help them to press for their rights, provided they understand what is available.

STATE BENEFITS

Ask what your rights are at your local DHSS office or Citizens' Advice Bureau. Very often you will find that some benefits also apply to non-pensioners. Financial help may come in the form of Supplementary Benefit, rent and rate rebates (Housing Benefit) and Attendance Allowance, as well as extra financial help through grants for insulation.

Supplementary Benefit

This is intended to help people on low incomes with savings of less than £3,000. It aims to provide a guaranteed minimum income and a person's entitlement to Supplementary Benefit is worked out by comparing needs with financial resources. The difference between the two is usually paid out weekly. This benefit is supposed to cover living expenses but many people, including pensioners, use the money for extra warmth.

An initial claim can be made by filling in a standard form (SB1) which you get from the post office or DHSS office. The address of your local DHSS office is in the telephone book under 'H' for Health and Social Security.

Heating Additions

People already on Supplementary Benefit who are over 65 are automatically eligible for a 'Heating Addition'. This is an extra weekly payment of around £2 a week, or something like £5 for people over 85. (It could be less than that if you have been on benefit for a long time.)

The Heating Addition is also available to people with conditions such as bronchitis, rheumatism or arthritis and those whose homes are particularly difficult to heat because of draught, damp or very large rooms. Housebound or disabled people should also be able to get the extra payment. Inform the DHSS if any of these conditions apply to you. (These additions are fixed sums and bear no relation to the actual size of your fuel bills.)

Single Payments

If a person is already on Supplementary Benefit, then he or she may be eligible for other benefits such as Single Payments. These are lump sums for items such as bedding, draughtproofing, hot water tank jackets, heaters and in some cases for partial double glazing. To claim these payments you must be on Supplementary Benefit, have less than £500 saved up and satisfy additional criteria for some specific items.

Post offices and DHSS offices have leaflets describing the money that can be claimed and forms. Make sure they give you all the forms that might be relevant, and if you find them difficult to get hold of or confusing, which they often are, seek advice. Some of the best advice comes from local Citizens' Advice Bureaux who deal with such matters every day. The address or phone number of your local CAB is in the telephone book.

Housing Benefit

Those who are not entitled to Supplementary Benefit may still be eligible for Housing Benefit, for which there is no limitation on the amount of savings you have. This is specifically for help towards rent and rates, but every little helps towards keeping warm.

People who have applied for Supplementary Benefit and just missed entitlement by a few pounds may be able to claim Housing Benefit Supplement. This entitles you to claim for the single payment mentioned above for bedding, draughtproofing and so on. If you look on your rent and rates statements, you will see whether this is already being given.

Grants for loft insulation

If you live in a council house, find out if there are any programmes planned for modernisation or insulation work on your home. If conditions are cold and draughty, perhaps the local tenants' association is already trying to get something done about it.

For most householders a loft insulation grant is usually

66 per cent of the cost of materials up to £69 maximum. For the elderly, severely disabled or for people on low incomes it may be possible to get 90 per cent of the cost paid, up to a maximum of £95.

Code of practice

If by any chance you cannot pay your bills at the end of a quarter the Gas and Electricity Boards have agreed on a code of practice. They will not disconnect the fuel supply of pensioners between the months of October and March unless they believe the money is being deliberately withheld.

If you are not a pensioner, but are blind, severely sick or disabled, or are receiving Supplementary Benefit, you may still be covered by the Code of Practice. Should either the Gas or Electricity Board send you notification that they are about to send someone round to disconnect, do not get upset. First get in touch with the board concerned or contact one of the advice centres, such as the Citizens' Advice Bureau or a local Neighbourhood Energy Action group. Act quickly as there is nearly always a solution if you do not leave things too late.

Paying bills

Pensioners and out-of-work families have the right to make arrangements to pay the bill over a period of time. There are various different arrangements to choose from.

1. Weekly or monthly payments. These payments consist of a fixed amount each week to pay off the debt, plus an amount based on an estimate of how much you are likely to spend on fuel over the next quarter. This is called the 'current consumption'.
2. You can have a coin-in-the-slot meter installed, which appeals to many people because you pay as you go and know where you stand. The meter can also be adjusted to collect arrears. However, it is an expensive way to pay your bills and inconvenient if you run out of the right sort of coins. There is also the

risk that the machine may be burgled.

3. If you are receiving Supplementary Benefit and get into debt, you may be able to join a scheme called 'fuel direct'. This means that the money you owe is deducted week by week from your benefit. It is best to contact the DHSS about this option.

8.
THE FUTURE

The Network for Alternative Technology and Technology Assessment (NATTA) predicts that supplies of oil and gas could run out in about 25 years' time at the present rate of consumption. That is about a million times faster than they are being created. If we are really running out of fossil fuels we shall have to find alternative sources of energy in order to keep warm in the future.

There are various options. Nuclear energy is already used in many countries, but it raises provocative and unanswered questions about the storage and disposal of waste from reactor plants. Recent accidents in America, Britain and, the worst so far, Russia should also make us cautious of putting all our eggs into the nuclear basket.

Other possible forms of energy are solar energy, wind power and wave power. Some of these are realistic options but much research is still needed to develop efficient and practical household systems.

SOLAR ENERGY

The sun's energy will last for many millions of years and causes no waste or pollution. It therefore makes sense to exploit the potential of solar heating now and not just in preparation for the future, to preserve the small supplies of coal, gas and oil which we have left. Compared with coal or nuclear power stations, solar energy is both safe and clean.

Its effectiveness as a heating source, however, is less certain. Before coal became cheap and plentiful, new houses were carefully sited towards the sun, so that living rooms had large south-facing windows. Such houses benefit from what's called 'passive' solar heating, as

opposed to 'active' solar heating which collects the heat
and recycles it. During the industrial revolution and
between the world wars, however, houses were built to
standardised designs and in urban lay-outs, without
thought for the weather or the sun. Today we have come
full circle and homes are once again being built with
passive solar heating in mind, and there are many projects
afoot to adapt homes to make use of the sun's rays.

In Britain, you can save some money using solar energy
to heat your water, but there is not enough sunlight to
heat it all throughout the year. Nor do we have enough
sun to cope with whole-house heating, so do not trust any
advertising which claims to.

PASSIVE SOLAR COLLECTION

Passive solar collection works in the same way as a greenhouse. The temperature inside the building rises higher than outside as the sun's energy passes through the glass and becomes trapped inside as heat. This heat circulates without escaping because glass lets strong radiated energy in from the sun, but will not let it out again. Likewise there is very little heat loss due to re-radiation from a well-insulated building or the inside of a room once it has been heated up by solar energy.

Gaining heat from the sun through ordinary windows is called passive solar heating because it uses no moving parts or extra equipment. Only the space immediately beneath the glass is heated. Any method of transferring the heat to other areas becomes 'active' solar heating.

To make the best use of solar energy, buildings must conform to certain rules. They should have large glass windows in south-facing walls. The heat generated can be circulated by convection in the surrounding well-insulated rooms. Many houses have sun rooms or sun spaces, consisting of a sort of greenhouse extension to a south or east face, attached to them. Others can be converted to passive solar collection by replacing the roof tiles with glass panels.

Fuel savings of up to 30 per cent have been reported, but Britain seems slow to catch on to passive solar collection. It requires a new approach to building design. Since it adds only one per cent to the cost of initial construction, passive solar collection features on a new home would pay for themselves in less than two years. With improved conduction and ventilation, and 30 per cent of heating requirements met by the sun, houses could be fitted with smaller heating systems and be just as comfortable.

Direct gain

Direct gain is the name given to a building design which makes the most of solar energy without adding to the building costs. No new materials or extraordinary construction practices are needed and new buildings can readily make use of passive solar heating.

The houses should have large south-facing windows to heat the living areas directly while the sun is shining. Any heat lost back through the glass at night and on cloudy days is never more than that gained. Internal thermal storage in brick walls soaks up the solar heat during the day and releases it at night. There should also be a controlled back-up heating system integrated with the passive solar design.

In Milton Keynes, 100 direct gain houses have been built and their performances compared to those of similar houses which do not use the sun's heat. With increased draughtproofing and insulation the heating bills of the solar houses were 40 per cent lower than the other houses. Just by using the sun's natural energy you can have high comfort, low bills and light sunny living spaces.

You do not have to have a new house to benefit from passive solar heating. Sun spaces in the form of conservatories and sun rooms can be added to many existing houses. Built against the south side of a house and taking the form of a lean-to, a glazed extension can be used for storage and in the summer may double as a study or extra living-room space. A lean-to addition covers a large area of wall and therefore prevents heat loss from that wall of the house. In sunny weather, the hot air filling the sun space warms a wall far more efficiently than if the sun was shining directly onto it.

When solar gains in a sun space are enough to raise the temperature above that inside the house, there are various methods of letting the warm air into other rooms. An air brick near the top of the lean-to (where the warmest air collects) lets the air in under the force of its own buoyancy, but a thermostatically controlled form of vent might be more effective. Alternatively, connecting doors or windows could be opened at opportune times.

All these methods depend on the specific conditions of your home. This is a new area for designers and research

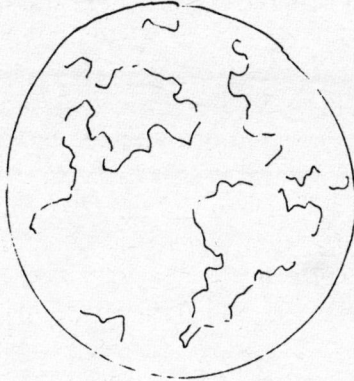

is still being done. With luck someone will come up with a
design which makes the transference of heat from the sun
space to the house simple and reliable. In any event there
is enough information to show that sun spaces can be a
cost effective and reliable source of extra heating.

Roof space

If the roof needs retiling or reslating, you might take the
opportunity of glazing all or part of the south-facing slope.
You would then have the benefit of a great deal of solar
heat collecting in the loft space which would otherwise re-
radiate back out to the sky. If you choose to glaze, you
could put in a flat plate collector beneath, which could
help to top up the heating for your water. Obviously this
costs more than a simple retiling job, but if your house
faces the right way to get the most sun, it might be
worthwhile.

Different glazing systems are available and firms will often do the fitting for you. You can, however, do the job yourself from inside the loft. Leave a trap door at one of the corners to enable you to poke your arms and head out when you need to wash the surface down. Make sure all the edges are well and permanently weatherproofed.

With the current state of knowledge, passive solar design cannot be the complete answer to home heating in Britain, but it can certainly be a cost effective aid to many energy needs.

ACTIVE SOLAR HEATING

'Active' collection occurs when special collectors are used to absorb energy from the sun and when some means of transferring the heat is incorporated into the system.

Flat plate collectors

The most common technique for active solar heating is the flat plate collector. There are now about 20,000 solar water heaters of this kind in Britain and the number is growing.

The sun heats the water as it circulates in a thin rectangular metal or plastic plate (rather like a radiator). The plate has a black surface so as to absorb radiation and is covered by glass to reduce the heat loss back from the plate. The back of the plate is heavily insulated to reduce heat loss further. Once heated the water can be circulated through a central heating system to heat living space or it may be stored in a tank to provide 'on tap' hot water. In both cases a water pump and storage tank are incorporated into the system.

There are two types of system to provide solar heated water:

The two tap system   This is a hot tap and a cold tap. When there is not enough solar heated water, an electric immersion heater or gas water heater is activated to make up the difference.

Three tap system On top of your conventional water system, you have a third solar tap which drains from a cylinder of entirely solar heated water.

In Britain there is not enough sunlight to meet all hot water needs throughout the year, but substantial savings in energy use are being achieved wherever these systems are used. Spectacular results can be achieved when active solar heating is used in combination with passive solar designs and where rigorous draught-proofing and insulation has been fitted. In some cases, an intermittent supplement of hot water supplied by a solar system can reduce the amount of gas or electricity used by up to 50 per cent.

Installing such a system is liable to be expensive and it will probably take about ten years to pay for itself. On the other hand, as fossil fuels become scarcer they will become more expensive, and solar energy may become a cheaper alternative over the years. The more solar heating systems that are in use (and as they become more popular the chance of advancing in solar technology increases) the longer the fossil fuels will last, and the more time there will be for developing alternative energy supplies.

Several companies are now offering solar heating systems and the Solar Trade Association has a code of conduct and a list of members. Nevertheless, companies do, predictably, employ sales techniques associated more with notorious double glazing salesmen and should always be treated with caution. Before committing yourself to any system or signing any piece of paper, check your position with the Solar Trade Association and get as much advice as you can about what sort of system you might have and whether it is really worth your while installing solar heating at all.

Points to consider
- Most systems take at least ten years to pay for themselves at present prices.
- Make sure the system you buy will last longer than

ten years — get a guarantee.

- To achieve the highest energy efficiency, you should reckon on one square metre of collector per person. Any more will probably give you lower savings.
- There should ideally be a solar pre-heating tank between the existing cold tank and the hot water cylinder. This should have a capacity of 50 litres per square metre of collector.
- Collectors are put in the most exposed place you can find and must therefore be tough enough to withstand freezing conditions, as well as high winds and rain. They can also reach very high temperatures in the summer, so a system must be well prepared to withstand all extremes.
- Solar panels are not as yet economical for house heating systems, though the possibilities are being looked at.

WIND POWER

For at least two thousand years windmills have been used for pumping water and grinding corn. These should be familiar to everyone even if only from pictures. They are tall structures with large sails fastened to a wheel fixed at the top. When the wind catches the sails it carries them round with great force, turning the wheel to grind the corn and so on. In East Anglia there are many old brick windmills with great wooden sails to catch the wind off the sea, and in Crete there is a whole valley of windmills with canvas sails.

Recent developments have resulted in windmills, called wind turbines or aerogenerators, which generate electricity. These are very large and have to be situated high on hills or by windy waters, often on coastlines.

Reliable equipment that fully exploits the power of the wind is usually very expensive. The energy has to be stored for when the wind drops and this means the use of costly, bulky batteries. The windmills have to be strong

enough to withstand strong winds — a toppling windmill is spectacular to watch but extremely dangerous. They are also very noisy and cause a good deal of vibration which prevents them being built near residential areas.

In Schiedam in Holland, modern windmills supply electric energy to surrounding factories and offices. Along the Niewe Watereweg, for instance, a 48-metre-high turbine generates about 300,000 kwh (kilowatt hours) a year. It weighs 40,000 kg and has two fibreglass reinforced rotor blades which feed the wind power to a 300 kw dynamo. The result is a constant electricity supply.

Less ambitious projects have also been successful. A relatively cheap, homespun version might supply electricity to the home of a competent enthusiast. On the whole, however, windmills or aerogenerators show potential for cheap electricity supplies only where the wind is strong and where the great towers can be at some distance from populated areas.

WAVE POWER

Wave power seems particularly relevant for an island country like Britain. Certain coastal areas provide ideal conditions for prolonged trapping of energy from waves. The Scottish and South West coasts, especially the Severn estuary, are probably the best sites.

The raft was designed by Sir Christopher Cockerell (who invented the hovercraft). It consists of two vessels calls pontoons. The first is divided into two sections which bob up and down with the waves. This movement drives a pump in the back pontoon which sucks in water and, under high pressure, drives it at a turbine. This turbine is the drive for the electricity producing generator. Whilst the production of electric power can successfully be achieved, the storage and transference of the power still presents a big problem.

The current method of transferring power is to make hydrogen gas on the vessel which can then be transported ashore and converted to electricity. There are dangers involved but it is hoped that these can be wiped out.

At present most government resources are going into nuclear power which is known to be dangerous and which will cause untold damage in the event of an accident. In the meantime, the more we, as individuals, conserve our resources, the longer our present fossil fuels will last and the better chance we have of encouraging safer alternatives.

USEFUL ADDRESSES

ADVISORY ORGANISATIONS

Monergy Saver Freepost
Newcastle-upon-Tyne
NE1 1BR
No stamp needed. They will deal with enquiries about
heating problems.

London Heatwise
165-167 New Kent Road
London SE17 4AG
Tel: 01-403 0845

The London Energy and Employment Network
99 Midland Road
London NW1 2AH
Tel: 01-387 4393
Leen is a special agency established to help tackle high
heating costs at home and work. **Leen** works alongside
local authorities, community groups, local enterprises and
tenants to provide new ideas and services and to publicise
and promote examples of good procedure. They have a list
of publications and videos.

Citizens' Advice Bureaux
See local telephone directory for address. Will help on any
consumer problem.

Energy Efficiency Office
Room 1312
Thames House South
Millbank
London SW1P 4QJ
Tel: 01-211 6326
Has a mass of leaflets on all forms of insulation and
energy saving in the home.

The Consumer Association
14 Buckingham Street
London WC2N 6DS
Publishes the magazine *Which?* and other books and
publications. Gives advice to members.

DRAUGHTPROOFING

Draughtproofing Advisory Association Ltd
PO Box 12
Haslemere
Surrey
Tel: 0428-54011

The Building Centre
26 Store Street
London WC1
Enquiry Service Tel: 0334-88499

Building Research Establishment
Bucknalls Lane
Garston
Watford WD2 7JR
Tel: 0923-674040

LOFT INSULATION AND LAGGING

Eurisol UK (Association of British Manufacturers of Mineral Insulating Fibres)
St Paul's House
Edison Road
Bromley
Kent BR2 0EP
Tel: 01-466 6719

The Building Centre
26 Store Street
London WC1
Enquiry Service Tel: 0334-88499

National Association of Loft Insulation Contractors
(As for Draughtproofing Advisory Association)

WALL INSULATION

National Cavity Insulation Association
(As for Draughtproofing Advisory Association)

The Cavity Foam Bureau
9-11 The Hayes
Cardiff CF1 1NU
Tel: 0222-388621

Expanded Polystyrene Cavity Insulation Association (EPCIA)
5 Belgrave Square
London SW1X 8PH
Tel: 01-235 9483

External Wall Insulation Association
(As for Draughtproofing Advisory Association)

Structural Insulation Association
24 Ormond Road
Richmond
Surrey TW10 6TH
Tel: 01-876 4415

DOUBLE GLAZING

Glass and Glazing Federation
6 Mount Row
London W1Y 6BY
Tel: 01-629 8334

HEATING SYSTEMS

Central Heating Energy Efficiency Confederation (CHEEC)
27 Langford Drive
Wootton
Northampton NN4 0JY

Heating and Ventilating Contractors Association (HVCA)
34 Palace Court
London W2 4JG

Solid Fuel Advisory Service
Look in local telephone book or phone Sunderland 73578 for local addresses.

HEATING CONTROLS

The HEVAC Control Manufacturers Association
Automatic Controls Group
Nicholson House
High Street
Maidenhead
Berks
Tel: 0628-34667/8

Association of Control Manufacturers
Leicester House
8 Leicester Street
London WC2H 2BN
Tel: 01-437 0678

ALTERNATIVE SYSTEMS

Network for Alternative Technology and Technology Assessment (NATTA)
c/o Alternative Technology Group
Faculty of Technology
The Open University
Walton Hall
Milton Keynes
Bucks

Solar Trade Association Ltd
19 Albemarle Street
London W1X 3HA

ABOUT THE AUTHOR

BARTY PHILLIPS is a popular and well-known writer on design and home affairs. Formerly home correspondent of *The Observer*, she is now a freelance journalist for *Good Housekeeping* and *The Sunday Times*.

She has appeared on television and featured on various radio programmes such as Tuesday Call. Among her numerous books are *Setting up Home, Conran and the Habitat Story* and *Doing up a Dump* (published by Macdonald).

When not writing at home, the renovated stables of a Georgian house in Hertfordshire, she is busy restoring the six-acre garden to its former glory.